Best Wishes,
   Kari and Layne

October 6, 1990

David DeAnne Lindsey
   & Jasper Raven

EASY COOKING
STEP·BY·STEP

BY BEV BENNETT
AND 17 OTHER LEADING FOOD WRITERS

BARRON'S

Woodbury, New York • London • Toronto • Sydney

All inquiries should be addressed to:

Barron's Educational Series, Inc.
113 Crossways Park Drive
Woodbury, New York 11797

International Standard Book No. 0-8120-5637-X

Library of Congress Catalog Card No. 85-1398

Library of Congress Cataloging in Publication Data
Main entry under title:

Easy Cooking Step-by-Step

   "Portions of this book previously published as
separate volumes in the Barron's Easy cooking series"—T.p.
verso.
   Includes index.
   1. Cookery. I. Barron's Educational Series, inc.
TX715.B4973 1985   641.5   85-1398
ISBN 0-8120-5637-X

Printed in Japan

5 6 7   9 8 7 6 5 4 3 2 1

CONTENTS

Such contradictory demands we make as cooks.

● We insist that no meal, no matter how extravagant, take more than an hour to prepare. (Well, maybe two or three hours, if it's a leisurely weekend and cooking is part of our recreation.) Although we love to get into the kitchen and work with food processors, mixers, blenders, and the array of exciting items in supermarkets, we love getting out just as much. Food is a part of our life, but it doesn't have to be a time-consuming part.

● We insist that speed not diminish the quality of our meals. Dinner shouldn't resemble a collision between the food processor and the rump roast. The food must be appetizing and fresh, and satisfy our creative natures.

● And, as still another criterion, we insist that recipes be easy. After all who wants to waste time stumbling through convoluted procedures?

Appropriately, we're evolving a new cooking style that allows us to bring all those dissimilar requirements together.

Now it is possible to have a meal that is quick, easy, affordable, attractive, and nutritious. And short of having food that cooks itself, that's some accomplishment!

This new style is what Easy Cooking Step-by-Step is all about. Recipes have flair, originality, and an inventive use of herbs and spices, but are simple enough for the beginning cook to follow.

It starts with culinary savvy.

Here is how to develop the food smarts that are the foundation to the new cooking style.

Be a Seasonal Shopper

Most of the recipes in the book use fresh fruits and vegetables. The best time to buy these ingredients is at their peak season. It is your assurance of having dishes that are at the height of flavor and most reasonably priced.

During the fall, cabbage, root vegetables, winter squash, spinach, leeks, apples, pears, grapes with seeds, cranberries, and pomegranates are readily available. In the winter, there's celery root,

jerusalem artichokes, fennel, avocados, mushrooms, and a wide assortment of citrus to add to menus.

Spring, of course, brings in a bouquet of asparagus, rhubarb, watercress, globe artichokes, apricots, strawberries, and pineapple. Everything gardens grow—fresh herbs, salad greens, tomatoes, summer squash, cherries, melons, seedless grapes, berries, peaches, plums, and nectarines—is for the picking in supermarkets or in the backyard.

Meat, poultry, fish, and seafood don't have the seasonal variances produce does. Many fish that were only available during a few months of the year are now in stores the year round because of fish farming. Mussels and trout are two examples of this. Still, your best chance for enjoying never-frozen turkey is in the Thanksgiving period; tender spring lamb, near Easter; and good oysters in the fall and winter months.

Plan your cooking seasonally, using dishes that focus on whatever produce, fish, and seafood is available.

For example, when spring asparagus are at their peak in April and May, prepare a stunning appetizer of Asparagus Roll-Ups (page 3), asparagus flavored with horseradish and cream cheese and encased in a smoked-salmon shell. When the first smelt catch hits the market in March or April, get out the skillet and make a mess of Fried Smelts (page 131).

Be a Flexible Shopper

Don't be afraid to alter the recipes in Easy Cooking Step-by-Step according to your needs and product availability.

Instead of shopping with a list of specifics, be open to ingredient changes. Look for a green vegetable and select what is most attractive; pick fish, fruit, poultry, and meat the same way.

If you love the tangy flavor of Asparagus Mimosa (page 297), but it's January and asparagus are as costly as caviar and tasting like potatoes, substitute broccoli. The recipe for Herbed Salmon Steaks (page 151) flecked with chives and parsley looks marvelous. However, if fresh salmon is exorbitant, switch to halibut. That's all part of the new cooking style.

Taste ingredients. Develop your palate. Choose the products you feel have the best taste. The quality of the raw ingredients influences a dish as much (if not more) than the time spent preparing it. You can make a superior salad dressing in minutes, simply by buying the best oil and vinegar you can afford. Good, sharp parmesan cheese makes Italian Drumsticks (page 175) especially well flavored.

Be an Economical Cook

Buy whole chickens—always. Even for a chicken breast recipe, whole chickens are more practical than chicken breasts. Usually, cut-up chickens are ten cents more per pound than whole ones, and chicken breasts cost double what whole chickens do per pound. With a good knife you can cut up a chicken in minutes. Freeze the leftovers to use later as the basis for a second, even third meal.

Learn to do more meat and fish cutting and boning yourself, Not only will you save money on the meat or fish portions, but you'll have scraps for soups and stocks.

Don't buy more food than you can use in a short time. Cheaper by the dozen isn't valid if the food spoils.

Love leftovers. A few bits of unfinished vegetables, a cup of cooked rice, and an untouched chicken breast are the makings of a nourishing soup or casserole. The French have raised the use of leftovers to a high art. They're considered great cooks.

Be an Adventuresome Cook

Explore new cooking techniques.

Invest in a wok and the implements to use with it. With its narrow base, high sides, and wide top, a wok is excellent for deep-frying foods with far less oil than a traditional deep-fryer requires. It is also a good utensil for steaming and for simmering. A wok is best suited however, for stir-frying. Ingredients are cut into small pieces and rapidly cooked with a little oil over very high heat and then flavored with a sauce. A typical stir-fry dish cooks in about 10 minutes. It's not only speedy, it's nutritious as well since the food is cooked so briefly with so little fat.

Don't limit stir-frying to Oriental cooking. It is marvelously efficient whenever you want to cook small pieces of food quickly to maintain the color and texture. There is a wonderful assortment of stir-fry recipes in Easy Cooking Step-by-Step.

Poaching foods in a simmering bath of seasoned water, broth, or wine is another cooking technique that will broaden your repertoire. It is the perfect way to cook a delicate dish such as Spinach-Stuffed Fillets with Shrimp Sauce (page 139) that would fall apart if cooked by another method.

Not only fish, but chicken and fruit can be poached in minutes. Foods often have more of their natural flavor and a lighter texture when poached rather than baked.

Sauces certainly enhance the taste of poached dishes, as in the succulent Poached Chicken With Red Pepper Sauce (page 179). But if you can stand to eliminate the cream and butter coatings, poaching provides the key to low fat, low calorie cooking.

Be a Good Menu Planner

Menu planning is a skill, rather than a science, and you can easily perfect it. Meals have changed considerably during the last few decades. Since people don't work as strenuously as in the past, there isn't the need—and rarely the desire—for heavy, multi-course meals. Everyone is more health conscious, and the very thought of soup, dinner rolls, salad, roast meat with dumplings, potatoes and gravy, followed by apple pie is enough to unhinge the bathroom scale.

A salad or vegetable; an entree such as meat, fish, poultry, eggs or cheese, and perhaps a starch like potatoes, pasta, or rice, is sufficient. Add a simple dessert if you like.

Occasionally you'll discover that a hearty bowl of soup, such as Shredded Vegetable and Pasta Soup (page 45) or Garbanzo and Sausage Soup (page 47) is all you crave. At the peak of summer a Spinach and Feta Salad (page 329) or Stuffed Tomatoes (page 335) will seem an ambrosial meal.

The trick to assembling a meal is to vary the colors, textures, and flavors of the dishes for variety. If you're serving poached fish as an entrée, a green vegetable would be preferable to mashed potatoes. When the main course is Spicy Chicken and Walnut Stir-Fry (page 171)—and the name says it all—balance the heat with a simple side dish of rice and a dazzling, but mild Roasted Red Pepper Salad (page 333).

Be an Organized Cook

As desirable as speed cooking is at 6 p.m. when the family roars for food, it can be an exhausting exercise. There are a couple of tricks to use for weeknight meals when you've got the energy level of an over-cooked spaghetti strand. As silly as they might sound, they do work.

First, if you plan to use the oven, preheat it the minute you walk in the door. (Yes, before you take off your coat or look at the mail.)

Second, if you plan to use any boiling hot water—for pasta, steamed vegetables, or poached fish—start a large, covered pot of water going instantly.

Then you can take off your coat and catch your breath as the kitchen preliminaries are taken care of.

Start the longest cooking dish, most likely the entree. If possible select something that will sit on top of the stove or in the oven with little tending. Meanwhile cook or assemble a salad or vegetable. Desserts generally can bake while the family eats dinner.

And that's all you need to start cooking.

Easy Cooking Step-by-Step will be your guide as you prepare delicious meals for yourself, your family, and friends.

It's a collection of great recipes from each menu category bound together in one book. The recipes are so varied, you'll find something suitable for any need, from a back-yard barbecue to the most formal dinner.

Choose from the Light Meals, Snacks, and Sandwiches chapter for lunches, picnics, or impromptu meals. The Fish and Shellfish, Poultry, Beef and Veal, and Pork and Lamb sections have dozens of recipes for every-day dinners.

Match appetizers, soups, salads, and desserts with one of the entrée selections for a special occasion.

For example, start with Asparagus Roll-Ups (page 3), follow with Broiled Tomato Soup (page 37), Grilled Sea Bass (page 127), Julienne Vegetable Sauté (page 315) and end with Raspberries Romanoff (page 361) for summer.

Blue Cheese Tartlets (page 15) make a rich start to a winter splurge. Brandied Apple Soup (page 57), Rack of Lamb with Tiny Potatoes (page 277), Chocolate Lace Cookies (page 401), and the best coffee possible complete the meal.

The book has special features you'll come to rely upon.

Even if you are a very experienced cook, you'll enjoy the step-by-step photos with each recipe. The pictures clarify any difficult aspects of preparation.

You'll see how easy it is to wrap soft brie cheese around an olive for the Brie-Wrapped Olives (page 9) appetizer; see how to turn Vegetarian Consomme with Lemon-Yogurt Dumplings (page 35) a rich, brown color by caramelizing sugar; discover the secret to peeling bell peppers for the Roasted Red Pepper Salad (page 333), and marvel at how Chinese rice sticks puff up in the Chinese Tossed Chicken Salad dish (page 343).

As restaurant chefs are fond of saying, ''we eat first with our eyes,'' and the stunning full-color photos of the finished dishes are a feast. They can inspire you to cook something new each night. If you want to encourage someone else to do the cooking, just leave the book open to one of the mouth-watering pictures; you'll quickly have help in the kitchen.

Each recipe includes both preparation time—when you'll have to attend to the dish, and cooking time—when you can start something else. Look over the cooking times of the various dishes in the meal. You'll be able to choose foods that work well together and eliminate the problem of not having everything ready at the same time.

Though the dishes are innovative, they use ingredients available in supermarkets throughout the country. When something special is required, a note will tell where to find the product or what to substitute.

Recipes also include nutritional data (more on this follows) which you'll find especially useful when watching calories. Although it wasn't intentional, many of the desserts have modest calorie counts.

Understanding the Recipe Analyses

The recipes in this book include data on protein, fat, sodium, carbohydrates, and potassium, as well as the number of calories (kcal) per serving. If you're looking for a meal that is high in protein, while low in calories, these figures should help you choose your recipes accordingly. However, the calculations are estimates and should be followed only in a very general way. No two pieces of round steak, for example, will have the exact same amount of fat or calories. Your cooking technique will also affect the nutrient data. If you are on a rigid diet, consult your physician. The analyses are based on the number of portions given as the yield for the recipe, but if the yield reads "4 to 6 servings," we indicate which number of servings was used to determine the final amounts.

Bev Bennett

APPETIZERS AND HORS D'OEUVRE

Asparagus Roll-Ups

YIELD

12 servings
(24 pieces)

Per serving (12)
calories 39, protein 2 g,
fat 3 g, sodium 463 mg,
carbohydrates .5 g,
potassium 40 mg

TIME

30 minutes preparation
1 hour chilling

INGREDIENTS

1 tablespoon minced fresh parsley
2 teaspoons well-drained prepared
   white horseradish
3 ounces cream cheese
6 pieces (2 by 4 inches) smoked
   salmon
6 asparagus spears, each 4 inches
   long, cooked

Cream together parsley, horseradish, and cream cheese.

Spread about 1 tablespoon of the cream cheese mixture over each salmon strip ①. Place asparagus over cream cheese on the long side ②. Fold or roll salmon over to enclose asparagus ③. Chill 1 hour.

Before serving, cut each strip into 4 1-inch pieces. Serve cold, with toothpicks.

NOTE If desired, place 3 salmon rolls on a lettuce-lined plate and serve as first course. (Makes 2 servings as a first course.)

Taramosalata in Pea Pods

YIELD

12 servings (40 to 50)

Per serving
calories 230, protein 5 g,
fat 20 g, sodium 318 mg,
carbohydrates 8 g,
potassium 108 mg

TIME

45 minutes preparation
1 hour chilling

INGREDIENTS

4 ounces carp-roe caviar (see note)
2 tablespoons cold water
1 cup fresh bread crumbs
4 tablespoons lemon juice
1 cup olive oil
¼ cup minced onion
1 small clove garlic, peeled and
    minced
1 tablespoon minced fresh dill
    (or 1 teaspoon dried)
Salt and black pepper to taste
40 to 50 fresh snow peas

In blender or food processor fitted with steel blade, place carp-roe caviar and cold water. Blend briefly. Add bread crumbs and lemon juice and blend briefly again. Trickle in oil as you would for making mayonnaise ①. When mixture is thick and oil is used, add onion, garlic, and dill and blend until smooth. Season very lightly with salt, if necessary, and add pepper to taste. Set aside.

Steam snow peas about 3 minutes, until they puff up and turn bright green (they will deflate again). When cool enough to handle, trim off stem end and strings ②. This will open peas. Fill each pea with ½ to 1 tablespoon taramosalata, depending on the size of the pea. This can be done by hand or with a pastry tube ③. Chill 1 hour. Serve cold.

NOTE Carp-roe caviar is available in jars in Greek food stores and is called tarama. If unavailable, substitute 4 ounces of the cheapest and strongest-flavored red caviar.

Fresh Vegetables with an Herbed Garlic Dip

YIELD

8 to 10 servings
(about 1¾ cups)

Per serving (9)
calories 219, protein 1 g,
fat 23 g, sodium 293 mg,
carbohydrates 2 g,
potassium 85 mg

TIME

15 minutes preparation

INGREDIENTS

3 ounces cream cheese
1 clove garlic
1 small onion
1 bunch fresh parsley
¼ teaspoon dried tarragon
3 tablespoons white wine vinegar
½ teaspoon salt
Several dashes white pepper
1 cup mayonnaise
Assorted fresh vegetables, washed
    and dried

About 30 minutes ahead, take cream cheese out of refrigerator to soften, or use a presoftened variety.

Peel and mince the garlic ①. Mince the onion and measure so you have 3 tablespoons ②. Chop the parsley ③ and measure; you should have about ¾ cup.

In a blender or food processor, mix all ingredients except mayonnaise and vegetables. Stir in mayonnaise and chill dip until ready to serve. Serve with crisp fresh vegetables.

Brie-Wrapped Olives

YIELD

12 servings (3 dozen)

Per serving
calories 205, protein 8 g,
fat 18 g, sodium 453 mg,
carbohydrates 1 g,
potassium 122 mg

TIME

25 minutes preparation
1 hour chilling

INGREDIENTS

1 pound ripe brie or camembert
  cheese
About 3 dozen small pimiento-stuffed
  green olives or pitted black olives
1 cup finely chopped pecans

Remove rind from cheese (either discard or save for another recipe) ①.

Pat olives dry. Shape about ½ tablespoon cheese around each olive ②. Place nuts on plate and roll each cheese ball in nuts to coat ③. Chill 1 hour before serving. Serve cold.

Nachos

YIELD

24 tostadas

Per nacho

calories 112, protein 6 g,
fat 7 g, sodium 230 mg,
carbohydrates 7 g,
potassium 70 mg

TIME

30 minutes preparation
5 minutes cooking

INGREDIENTS

1 small package (6 ounces) tostadas
24 ¼-inch-thick squares monterey
  jack, or 2 cups coarsely grated
  mixture of monterey jack and cheddar
  cheeses
24 slices jalapeño peppers, or to taste
Guacamole (see below)
2 cups refried pinto beans, heated
Sour cream

1 tomato, chopped
Pitted black olives
1 pound chorizo sausage, fried, drained,
  and crumbled

Place tostadas on a large, ovenproof platter. Evenly distribute cheese over top and sprinkle with jalapeño slices to taste ①.

Place tostadas under broiler until cheese melts. Then place guacamole in center of nachos ②, put a scoop of refried beans at either end ③, garnish with sour cream and a few sprinkles of extra cheese. Scatter chopped tomato over top of guacamole. Sprinkle olives over tostadas and encircle dish with chorizo or chile.

TO MAKE GUACAMOLE Half 2 ripe avocados and scoop out flesh into a 1-quart bowl. Cut with a knife and a fork into ½-inch cubes. Add ½ a fresh tomato, finely chopped; 2 teaspoons lime or lemon juice; 2 chopped green onions; 1 minced clove of garlic; ½ teaspoon salt; and 1 fresh, finely minced jalapeño pepper. Stir. Prepare just before eating.

Hot-Peppered Cheese Dip

YIELD

6 to 8 servings
(about 1 cup)

Per serving (6)
calories 249, protein 14 g,
fat 20 g, sodium 357 mg,
carbohydrates 2 g,
potassium 57 mg

TIME

10 minutes preparation
5 minutes cooking

INGREDIENTS

1 tablespoon butter
1 large clove garlic, peeled and
  minced
2 cups grated aged cheddar cheese
1 cup grated monterey jack cheese
3 tablespoons beer
½ teaspoon Worcestershire sauce
3 seeded and chopped green chilies
  (or to taste)
Hot pepper sauce
Corn tortillas or corn chips

In a nonstick saucepan, melt butter and sauté garlic until soft ①. Do not allow to brown or garlic will take on a bitter taste. Add cheeses and cook, stirring ②, over medium heat until cheeses are melted. Stir in remaining ingredients ③, adding pepper sauce until cheese has a slightly spicy taste.

Serve dip hot with deep-fried corn tortillas or crispy corn chips. This dip can be made in advance and reheated over a low flame, stirring constantly.

NOTE Unless it is to be consumed immediately, it is best to keep this hot cheese dip warm in a chafing dish over a low heat.

Blue Cheese Tartlets

YIELD

6 servings
(12 tartlets)

Per serving
calories 347, protein 10 g,
fat 27 g, sodium 507 mg,
carbohydrates 14 g,
potassium 100 mg

TIME

50 minutes preparation
25 minutes cooking

INGREDIENTS

Pastry for 1 9-inch pie crust (use
    favorite recipe)
6 tablespoons blue cheese, crumbled
2 whole eggs
1/2 cup heavy cream
1/4 cup milk
4 ounces mild cheese (monterey jack
    or brick), grated
1/4 teaspoon ground nutmeg
1/4 teaspoon salt

Preheat oven to 400 degrees.

Roll out pastry on floured board, to form a 12-inch circle. Using a 3-inch cutter, cut rounds of dough. By reworking dough scraps there should be 12 rounds. Grease the back of a 12-cup muffin pan. Fit rounds onto pan and part way up sides of cups, pressing lightly to seal ①. Bake for 10 minutes. If pastry has puffed up, press down lightly. Set aside to cool.

Reduce oven temperature to 350 degrees.

Remove pastry shells from backs of muffin pan and place upright on cookie sheet. Place 1/2 tablespoon of blue cheese in bottom of each shell ②. Combine eggs, cream, milk, grated cheese, nutmeg, and salt. Divide mixture among shells, pouring almost to the top ③. Don't overfill, as cheese mixture will rise during baking. There may be some leftover filling. Place filled shells in oven and bake for 15 minutes or until lightly browned and firm. Serve hot or tepid.

Curry-Stuffed Wontons

YIELD

6 to 8 servings
(20 wontons)

Per serving (6)
calories 269, protein 6 g,
fat 19 g, sodium 124 mg,
carbohydrates 16 g,
potassium 91 mg

TIME

15 minutes preparation
10 minutes cooking

INGREDIENTS

Oil for deep-frying
1 package (8 ounces) cream cheese
20 wonton wrappers
5 teaspoons chopped scallions, both
    white and green parts
Curry powder
1 whole egg, beaten
Soy sauce or sweet and sour sauce
    for dipping

Heat oil to 350 degrees.

Divide cream cheese into 20 equal parts. Place a cream cheese cube on top of each wonton wrapper. Top each with about ¼ teaspoon scallion and a dash or 2 of curry powder ①. Brush 2 adjacent sides of each wrapper with beaten egg and fold wrapper over to seal into a triangular shape ②.

Deep-fry wontons in hot oil until golden ③. Drain on paper towel. Serve hot with a bowl of soy sauce or commercially made sweet and sour sauce on the side.

Grape Leaves Stuffed with Goat Cheese

YIELD

6 servings

Per serving
calories 220, protein 4 g,
fat 14 g, sodium 219 mg,
carbohydrates 18 g,
potassium 205 mg

TIME

35 minutes preparation
10 minutes cooking

INGREDIENTS

1 package (7 ounces) mild goat
   cheese, or 5 ounces goat cheese
   plus 2 ounces softened cream
   cheese
1 tablespoon minced chives
1 tablespoon beaten egg
Coarsely ground black pepper
12 large grape leaves
Olive oil

Preheat oven to 350 degrees.

Cream together cheese, chives, egg, and pepper to taste.

Wash grape leaves and pat dry. Remove stems ①. Working with one leaf at a time, place 1 rounded tablespoon of the cheese mixture at stem end of each leaf ②. Roll up tightly, tucking ends in to form a cigar shape. Place rolls, open end down, on a greased baking sheet ③. Brush with olive oil. Bake for 10 minutes. Serve hot or tepid.

NOTE Grape leaves are available in jars in Greek or Middle Eastern food stores.

Dilled Salmon Terrine

YIELD

Serves 6

Per serving
*calories 405, protein 28 g,
fat 13 g, sodium 190 mg,
carbohydrates 2 g,
potassium 617 mg*

TIME

15 minutes preparation
2 hours chilling
30 minutes cooking

INGREDIENTS

1½ pounds boneless skinless salmon
1 egg + 1 extra white
Salt and freshly ground black pepper
   to taste
Squeeze of lemon juice
1 cup heavy cream
Large handful fresh dill sprigs, finely
   chopped
Boston or bibb lettuce for serving

Set the oven at 325 degrees.

Cut the salmon into small pieces and work them with the egg and extra white in a food processor until they are quite smooth. Add salt, pepper, and lemon juice and process just to combine. Pour the heavy cream through the feed tube and process to mix thoroughly, but turn off the machine as soon as the cream is incorporated. Transfer the mixture to a bowl, stir in the dill (reserving a few sprigs for garnish) and set aside.

Butter a 1-quart loaf pan and line the bottom and sides with foil cut to fit it ①. Butter the foil and spoon the fish mixture into the pan, pressing it down well ②. Bang the pan on the counter to settle any air pockets and cut a piece of foil to seal the top. Butter it and press it buttered side down onto the terrine.

Set the loaf pan in a roasting pan and pour enough boiling water to come halfway up the sides of the loaf pan ③. Bake the terrine for 30 minutes or until the fish feels firm when pressed on the top with a fingertip.

Remove the loaf pan from the water and let it cool off slightly. Refrigerate for 2 hours or until cold.

To serve, line 6 salad plates with some lettuce. Cut the terrine into thick slices and arrange 1 on each plate. Garnish the slice with some reserved dill sprigs and serve at once as an appetizer with buttered toast.

Baked Clams

YIELD

Serves 6

Per serving
calories 324, protein 11 g,
fat 22 g, sodium 385 mg,
carbohydrates 21 g,
potassium 156 mg

TIME

25 minutes preparation
10 minutes cooking

INGREDIENTS

18 cherrystone clams
1½ cups unseasoned bread crumbs
2 cloves garlic, finely minced
2 tablespoons finely chopped Italian
    (flat) parsley
Freshly ground pepper
Salt
½ teaspoon oregano
½ cup olive oil
4 tablespoons parmesan cheese

Wash clams and shuck them ①. Remove clam meat, drain, and chop fine ②. Wash 18 shell halves and set them aside. Preheat the oven to 450 degrees.

Divide the clam meat among the 18 shells. Place on a cookie sheet.

In a medium bowl combine bread crumbs, garlic, parsley, pepper, salt, and oregano. Add sufficient olive oil to hold mixture together. Divide mixture among shells, covering chopped clams completely ③. Sprinkle parmesan cheese over bread crumb mixture.

Bake clams in hot oven for 10 minutes. Run under broiler for a few seconds to brown. Serve as an appetizer, with lemon wedges if desired.

Smoked Fish Pâté

YIELD

Serves 6

Per serving
calories 153, protein 4 g,
fat 15 g, sodium 1179 mg,
potassium 34 mg

TIME

15 minutes preparation
1 hour chilling

INGREDIENTS

2 smoked trout (whole or boned) or
    2 smoked mackerel
½ cup unsalted butter, at room
    temperature
Freshly ground black pepper to taste
1 large sprig flat leaf parsley for
    decoration

If necessary, skin the trout or mackerel ①, discarding the heads and tails. Pull the flesh from the bones ② and run your fingers down the fillets to feel for any of the tiny bones hiding there. Pile the boned fillets into a food processor or blender and work them with the butter and black pepper until completely smooth.

Pack the pâté into a 3-cup crock or bowl and smooth the top with a metal palette knife. "Pleat" the top with a small palette knife so the surface looks like a bicycle wheel ③. Cover with plastic wrap and chill 1 hour.

Just before serving, let the pâté sit out for 10 minutes to soften slightly, then tuck the parsley sprig into the center of the pâté and pass triangles of dry toast separately.

Chicken Triangles

YIELD

12 servings
(24 triangles)

Per serving
calories 351, protein 17 g,
fat 19 g, sodium 268 mg,
carbohydrates 26 g,
potassium 159 mg

TIME

1 hour, 15 minutes
preparation
20 minutes cooking

INGREDIENTS

1 cup butter, melted
3 eggs, beaten
3 cups chopped cooked boneless
 chicken breast
1/4 teaspoon saffron dissolved in
 1 tablespoon chicken broth
 (if desired, just use the broth)
1/4 teaspoon ground coriander
1/2 teaspoon ground nutmeg
3/4 teaspoon ground gingerroot

1 1/2 teaspoons ground cinnamon
3 tablespoons sugar
1/4 cup light or dark raisins
1/4 cup pine nuts
Salt and freshly ground black pepper
16 sheets phyllo dough

Place 2 tablespoons melted butter in top of double boiler. Add beaten eggs and cook, stirring often, until mixture resembles slightly underdone scrambled eggs. Stir in chicken. Add saffron mixture, along with coriander, nutmeg, ginger, 1 teaspoon cinnamon, 1 tablespoon sugar, raisins, pine nuts, and salt and pepper to taste. Mix well.

Preheat oven to 350 degrees.

Lay 2 sheets of phyllo dough, one on top of the other, on board or cookie sheet (keep remaining 14 covered with slightly damp cloth). Brush generously with melted butter. Cut into 3 vertical strips ①. Place a heaping tablespoon of the chicken mixture in corner of one strip and fold into triangle, then continue folding in triangles all the way up the strip ②. Trim off excess. Press edges of dough in to seal using more butter ③. Place triangle on ungreased cookie sheet.

Repeat making triangles with remaining 2 strips. Then repeat the entire process 7 more times (using 2 sheets of phyllo for each, cutting each into 3 strips). You'll have 24 triangles in all.

Mix together remaining 2 tablespoons sugar and remaining 1/2 teaspoon cinnamon. Brush triangles with remaining butter and sprinkle with sugar-cinnamon mixture. Bake for 20 minutes or until golden brown. Serve hot or tepid.

Sirloin Teriyaki

YIELD

8 to 12 servings

Per serving (8)
calories 367, protein 20 g,
fat 26 g, sodium 2024 mg,
carbohydrates 10 g,
potassium 351 mg

TIME

15 minutes preparation
2 hours marinating
3 to 8 minutes cooking

INGREDIENTS

2 pounds boneless sirloin
¾ cup pineapple juice
¾ cup soy sauce
2 tablespoons honey
1 clove garlic, peeled and mashed
Lots of fresh-cracked black pepper
    (about 1 teaspoon or to taste)

Cut steak into ¼-inch-thick slices ①. Combine pineapple juice, soy sauce, honey, garlic, and pepper. Add sirloin ② and marinate at least 2 hours in the refrigerator.

Soak bamboo skewers in cold water for 30 minutes. Thread beef slices onto skewers ③ and broil (either over hot coals or in stove broiler) until beef is cooked to desired doneness. Return beef to marinade and serve either warm or tepid.

Samosas

YIELD

8 to 12 servings
(about 34 samosas)

Per serving (8)
calories 327, protein 5 g,
fat 23 g, sodium 373 mg,
carbohydrates 23 g,
potassium 110 mg

TIME

30 minutes preparation
25 minutes cooking

INGREDIENTS

1/3 cup chopped onion
1 tablespoon butter
1 tablespoon curry powder
1/2 teaspoon paprika
1/4 teaspoon salt
1/2 teaspoon ground cinnamon
5 tablespoons heavy cream
1/2 cup cooked ground lamb or beef,
    or cooked and chopped potato
2 tablespoons raisins

2 tablespoons chopped walnuts
Pastry for 2 9-inch pie crusts (use
    favorite recipe)
1 egg white, beaten

Preheat oven to 350 degrees. Sauté the onion in butter until onion is soft. Add curry powder, paprika, salt, and cinnamon and cook for 30 seconds, stirring constantly. Add cream and cook until it just begins to thicken, stirring constantly ①. Add cooked meat or potatoes, raisins, and walnuts and continue cooking until mixture is almost dry. Let sit for 10 minutes to cool.

Roll out pastry and cut into rounds that are 2½ inches in diameter ②. Place about 1 teaspoon of filling into center of each round and pinch edges of dough together to form half circles ③. Repeat until all filling is used, using a little egg white to help seal shut if necessary. Brush each samosa with egg white and bake for 25 minutes or until golden. Serve hot or tepid.

SOUPS

Vegetarian Consomme with Lemon-Yogurt Dumplings

YIELD

6 to 8 servings

Per serving (6)

calories 211, protein 7 g, fat 3 g, sodium 527 mg, carbohydrates 41 g, potassium 534 mg

TIME

20 minutes preparation
1 hour, 50 minutes cooking

INGREDIENTS

1 large tomato
1 turnip
2 onions
2 green peppers
3 carrots
1 large stalk celery, with leaves
1 cup shredded lettuce
1 apple
1/4 cup chopped fresh parsley
3 tablespoons chopped fresh dill
1 tablespoon sweet paprika
Salt and freshly ground pepper

DUMPLINGS

2 cups all-purpose flour
2 1/2 tablespoons baking powder
Salt
2 eggs
1 container (8 ounces) plain yogurt
2 tablespoons chopped fresh chervil or parsley
1 1/2 teaspoons grated lemon peel
2 teaspoons lemon juice
1–3 tablespoons milk

Do not peel the vegetables or the apple—just rinse them off, cut up into big chunks, and place in soup kettle. Add the parsley, dill, paprika, egg shells from dumpling ingredients, and 3 quarts cold water. Bring to a boil; skim top, if necessary. Reduce heat, cover, and simmer for 1½ hours.

Strain broth through a sieve lined with a double layer of cheesecloth. Press down on the ingredients in the sieve with the back of a spoon to remove all the liquid. If storing, ladle into glass jars while hot. Cover and refrigerate right away. If you are going to serve now, with dumplings, then keep hot while you prepare them.

Combine all dry ingredients in top of a sifter and sift into a large bowl. Lightly beat eggs with yogurt, herbs, lemon peel, and juice. Mix with flour and add 1 to 3 tablespoons of milk to form moist batter ①. (It should not be runny, but heavy enough to drop off tip of spoon.) When adding to soup, drop from tablespoon to form 10 to 12 mounds spread over the surface of the soup to allow for swelling ②. Cover and cook 20 minutes.

NOTE For a soup with a rich, dark color, melt 1 tablespoon of sugar in a heavy enamel saucepan over a very low heat until it is burned black ③. Let cool completely! This is very important. Hot sugar when mixed with cold water can blow up. When cool, gradually add 1 cup of cold water and cook, stirring constantly, until liquid turns a rich brown. Pour into soup kettle. This liquid does not flavor the soup, as the extreme heat destroys the sweetness of the sugar, but it gives the soup a nice tone.

Broiled Tomato Soup

YIELD

6 servings

Per serving
calories 444, protein 10 g,
fat 39 g, sodium 789 mg,
carbohydrates 17 g, potassium
727 mg

TIME

30 minutes preparation
45 minutes cooking

INGREDIENTS

24 ripe plum tomatoes or 1 can
    (35 ounces) Italian peeled
    tomatoes, chopped
1/2 cup butter
2 tablespoons olive oil
1 large red onion, finely diced
1 small green pepper, seeded and
    finely diced
1 teaspoon each fresh chopped dill,
    parsley, basil; or 1/2 teaspoon dried
    of these herbs

1/4 cup tomato paste
2 tablespoons flour
4 cups chicken stock
2 tablespoons brown sugar (optional)
Salt and freshly ground pepper
1/2 pint heavy cream
3/4 cup freshly ground parmesan
    cheese

Plunge fresh tomatoes in boiling water for a few seconds. Remove. Use paring knife to remove skin ①. Cut into large dice and set aside.

Melt butter with oil in large, heavy saucepan over medium heat. Add onion and pepper and sauté until transparent, stirring occasionally but do not brown. Add tomatoes, herbs, and tomato paste and simmer uncovered slowly for 10 to 12 minutes, stirring often.

Blend flour with 1/4 cup of chicken broth to form a thick mixture. Add to remaining broth along with sugar (if desired) and stir into simmering tomato mixture ②. Bring to a boil, add salt and pepper to taste. Reduce to simmer and continue simmering uncovered for 30 minutes. Stir often to prevent burning. Turn off heat. Cool soup slightly.

Preheat the broiler. Transfer cooled soup to blender in batches and purée. When the entire mixture has been puréed, return to saucepan. Heat but *do not boil*. Turn off heat. Cover soup to keep warm.

Whip cream until stiff and gradually fold in all but 3 tablespoons of the cheese ③. Transfer soup to a broiler-proof casserole. Top with dollops of whipped cream. Sprinkle remaining cheese on top. Broil 6 inches from flame for 30 to 60 seconds. Do not burn. Serve right away. Also good as a cold soup. Do not broil and top with the whipped cream and cheese or yogurt or sour cream and dill.

Potage Saint-Germain

YIELD

4 servings

Per serving
calories 175, protein 12 g,
fat 3 g, sodium 374 mg,
carbohydrates 24 g,
potassium 530 mg

TIME

10 minutes preparation
10 minutes cooking

INGREDIENTS

1 tablespoon butter
1 carrot, peeled and diced
2–3 scallions, thinly sliced
1 tablespoon flour
1 can (13 ounces) evaporated skim
  milk
½ cup chicken broth
1 package (10 ounces) frozen petite
  peas, thawed
1–2 tablespoons dry sherry
Minced fresh parsley
Lemon slices

In a 2-quart saucepan, melt butter and sauté carrot and scallions ①. Add flour and cook, stirring, until foamy ②. Add the evaporated milk and the broth and bring to a boil, stirring occasionally. Add peas, reduce heat, and simmer until carrots are tender, about 6 to 8 minutes.

Whirl the soup in a blender, a portion at a time, until smooth (or force through a food mill or sieve) ③. Return purée to the pan, stir in the sherry to taste, and heat through. Serve hot or cold, garnished with minced parsley and lemon slices.

NOTE This is a light soup ideal as an hors d'oeuvre or first course.

Corn and Pumpkin Chowder

YIELD

6 to 8 servings

Per serving (6)
calories 695, protein 12 g,
fat 56 g, sodium 1058 mg,
carbohydrates 43 g,
potassium 709 mg

TIME

15 minutes preparation
45 minutes cooking

INGREDIENTS

½ cup butter
4 leeks or 2 onions, trimmed and
  chopped
½ cup all-purpose flour
6 to 8 ears corn, kernels cut off
2 cups cooked pumpkin
1½ cups chicken broth
1 teaspoon salt
½ pound bacon, cooked and crumbled
¼ teaspoon ground allspice
Few fresh grinds of black pepper
1 quart light cream

Melt butter in a soup kettle and cook the leeks until soft ①. Add the flour ②, corn, pumpkin, broth, and salt and simmer over low to moderate heat for about 10 minutes. Add bacon and mix.

Pour half the chowder into a blender or food processor ③ and mix until smooth. Return mixture to soup kettle, stir, and simmer 30 minutes. Add allspice, pepper, and cream. Heat 2 or 3 minutes more until completely heated, then serve.

Provincetown Kale Soup

YIELD

6 to 8 servings

Per serving (6)
calories 477, protein 22 g,
fat 32 g, sodium 3195 mg,
carbohydrates 27 g,
potassium 1076 mg

TIME

20 minutes preparation
1½ hours cooking

INGREDIENTS

1 cup canned kidney beans
1 large onion, chopped
1 pound spicy sausage (linguica or
    chorizo)
1 tablespoon salt
½ teaspoon black pepper
¼ cup chopped green cabbage
1 medium carrot, scraped and sliced
1 tablespoon vinegar
2½ quarts beef stock or water

1 pound kale, washed and chopped
2 cups peeled and cubed potatoes
Grated sharp cheese (optional)

Combine all ingredients except kale, potatoes and cheese, bring to a boil, then lower heat and simmer 1 hour. Remove sausage ①; chop or slice it ② and return to kettle.

Add kale ③ and simmer 30 minutes, or slightly more until kale is soft. About 10 minutes before kale is finished, add potatoes and cook. Taste for seasoning and add more salt if desired. Serve with grated cheese to sprinkle on top.

Shredded Vegetable and Pasta Soup

YIELD

Serves 4

Per serving
calories 425, protein 23 g,
fat 25 g, sodium 1545 mg,
carbohydrates 25 g,
potassium 792 mg

TIME

10 minutes preparation
15 minutes cooking

INGREDIENTS

3 scallions, trimmed at both ends
3 medium zucchini
3 medium carrots
4 tablespoons butter
1/4 pound baked ham, thickly sliced
4 cups chicken stock
1/3 cup orzo pasta or 3/4 cup fusilli
(corkscrew) pasta
1 cup freshly grated parmesan cheese
for serving

Slice the scallions and set aside ①. Shred the zucchini and carrots ②. Melt the butter in a large saucepan and cook the scallions for 3 minutes over a low heat. Add the zucchini and carrots ③ and continue cooking 5 minutes, stirring once or twice, until the zucchini begin to release their liquid.

Cut the ham into matchstick pieces and add to the vegetables with the chicken stock. Bring to a boil, cover, and simmer gently for 5 minutes.

Meanwhile, cook the orzo or fusilli in plenty of boiling salted water for 4 minutes for the orzo or 8 minutes for the fusilli or until tender. Drain and add to the soup. Reheat to boiling and serve sprinkled with parmesan cheese. Pass garlic bread separately.

Garbanzo and Sausage Soup

YIELD

6 servings

Per serving
calories 411, protein 26 g,
fat 20 g, sodium 2310 mg,
carbohydrates 30 g, potassium
727 mg

TIME

10 minutes preparation
2 hours cooking

INGREDIENTS

3 quarts beef broth
2 meaty ham hocks
1 large onion, chopped
1 bay leaf
1 pound chorizo or Italian sweet
   sausages, in ½-inch slices
4–6 cloves garlic, thinly sliced
2 cans (16 ounces each) garbanzo
   beans, with liquid, or ½ pound dry,
   soaked and cooked until tender
   with ½ cup cooking liquid

2 carrots, thinly sliced
½ small head cabbage, shredded
2 stalks celery (with leaves), thinly
   sliced
¼ teaspoon Tabasco
½ teaspoon ground sage
Salt and freshly ground pepper

Combine broth, hocks, onion, and bay leaf in a large pot and bring to a boil. Reduce heat, cover, and simmer for 1 to 1½ hours until meat is tender. Remove hocks and set aside to cool.

Brown sausages lightly in a medium skillet ① and then transfer them to broth. Drain off all but 1 tablespoon of fat in skillet ②, then add garlic and cook over low heat until golden. Transfer to broth. Add the beans and liquid to the broth, along with carrots, cabbage, and celery. Simmer 20 minutes or until vegetables are tender.

While soup simmers, cut meat from ham hocks ③. Skim the fat from broth and stir in ham pieces and the seasonings. Discard bay leaf and serve.

Quick Lunchtime Chowder

YIELD

1 serving

Per serving
calories 584, protein 44 g,
fat 34 g, sodium 2487 mg,
carbohydrates 25 g, potassium
915 mg

TIME

5 minutes preparation
10 minutes cooking

INGREDIENTS

2 tablespoons olive oil
1/4 cup chopped shallots
1 can (3 ounces) water-packed tuna,
    drained
1 teaspoon each: dried chervil and dill
1 1/2 cups vegetable stock
1/4 cup finely diced potato
1/4 cup canned tiny peas
1/4 cup finely diced carrot
1/2 cup creamed cottage cheese

Place oil in a saucepan and heat. Add the shallots and sauté for 2 to 3 minutes until softened. Add tuna, chervil, and dill and cook, stirring to blend. Stir in stock ① and vegetables. Cover and simmer for 5 minutes, then remove from heat. Blend half the cottage cheese with 3 to 4 tablespoons of hot soup ② and mix well before blending back into the soup ③. Heat the chowder, but do not boil.

NOTE Fill a thermos with this soup and take it to the office for a change from sandwiches.

Basic Chicken Soup

YIELD

8 servings

Per serving (stock only)
calories 115, protein 3 g,
fat 5 g, sodium 845 mg,
carbohydrates 15 g, potassium
392 mg

TIME

15 minutes preparation
3 hours cooking

INGREDIENTS

4 pounds chicken necks, backs, wings,
   feet, and 2–3 gizzards
4 quarts cold water
1 onion, stuck with 3–4 whole cloves
2 stalks celery, cut up with leaves
1 carrot, rinsed and diced

1 small parsnip, rinsed and diced
6 parsley stems and leaves
1 bay leaf
¼ teaspoon ground thyme
10 whole peppercorns
1 tablespoon salt

Rinse off chicken parts and place in a 6- to 8-quart kettle. Add other ingredients. Bring to a boil over medium heat, skim off foam with a large kitchen spoon ①, and simmer slowly uncovered, with bubbles rising from bottom. Continue to simmer 2½ to 3 hours or until liquid is reduced by half. Skim off foam from time to time, if necessary.

Strain soup through fine sieve lined with 2 layers of cheesecloth ②, pressing down on vegetables to remove all liquid ③. Discard vegetables and spices. When chicken pieces are cool enough to handle, remove skin and bones. Save any shreds of chicken for the soup. Soup is now ready to serve with rice, noodles, or kasha cooked according to package directions. Or store in refrigerator or freeze for later use.

To clarify, allow 1 egg white and 1 shell for each quart of soup. Place soup over low heat and add lightly beaten egg white and crumbled shell. Bring to boil, stirring constantly, and boil 2 minutes. Add 1 tablespoon ice water and remove from heat. Set aside for 5 to 6 minutes, then strain to remove shells.

BRAZILIAN CHICKEN SOUP Add ¼ cup long-grain rice to hot soup. Cook 20 minutes or until rice is tender. Add 1 small tomato (peeled, seeded, and chopped), 1 teaspoon each chopped fresh chives and parsley, and 1 tablespoon chopped fresh mint. Serve.

ITALIAN CHICKEN SOUP Add 1½ cups small pasta shells to hot soup and cook 5 to 8 minutes. Add 3 cups shredded escarole and ¼ teaspoon fennel seeds. Cook 5 minutes.

Petite Marmite

YIELD

4 servings

Per serving (soup and meat)

calories 577, protein 42 g, fat 37 g, sodium 670 mg, carbohydrates 16 g, potassium 887 mg

TIME

20 minutes preparation
3 hours cooking

INGREDIENTS

4 leeks
2–3 pounds beef marrow bones and veal knuckle bone
2 pounds boneless chuck
1 stalk celery (leaves removed), cut in 1-inch pieces
2 carrots, in 1-inch slices
1 small turnip, in 1-inch dice

1 bouquet garni (1 peeled clove garlic, cut in half lengthwise; 1 bay leaf; 3 sprigs fresh parsley; 10 peppercorns; 2 sprigs fresh chervil or 1 dried sprig—all tied in cheesecloth bag)
Salt

Preheat oven to 325 degrees.

Trim roots off leeks. Cut away and discard half the green parts ①. Cut leeks in half lengthwise and then into quarters lengthwise ②. Rinse well to remove all sand, separating the leeks gently under the water ③. Clean but try to keep vegetable intact as much as possible.

In a deep kettle or ovenproof casserole, cover bones with cold water and bring to a boil on top of the stove. Skim off any foam with large kitchen spoon. Add leeks, meat, and remaining ingredients and bring to a boil again. Skim off any foam.

Remove kettle from heat and transfer to oven. Cover and cook for 2½ to 3 hours or until meat is tender. Remove meat and vegetables and reserve. Discard bones. Strain broth through a sieve lined with a double layer of cheesecloth, pressing down on bouquet garni to remove all the juices. Discard.

Serve the strained broth as a first course with sliced meat and vegetables to follow. Or refrigerate or freeze the strained broth immediately in glass jars to use as a base for other soups and stews. Wrap the meat separately to freeze.

Highland Broth

YIELD

4 to 6 servings

Per serving (4)
*calories 416, protein 40 g,
fat 17 g, sodium 270 mg,
carbohydrates 25 g,
potassium 1143 mg*

TIME

30 minutes preparation
2 hours, 15 minutes
cooking

INGREDIENTS

2½ pounds stewing lamb (breast or
    neck), with bones
3 lean, meaty beef shortribs
6 cups water, or 3 cups canned
    chicken broth mixed with 3 cups
    water
1 large onion, minced
2 large carrots, pared and grated
3 stalks celery, trimmed and diced
1 leek, trimmed, washed, and sliced
1 parsnip, pared and diced

¼ cup barley, rinsed and drained
1 small bay leaf
3 tablespoons chopped fresh parsley
½ teaspoon dried leaf thyme
Salt and pepper to taste

Rinse lamb and shortribs. Place meat in a kettle or saucepan, add water, cover, bring to a boil, and simmer for 1 hour. Add remaining ingredients, cover again, and simmer an additional hour.

Remove meat from kettle; let cool slightly. Take meat off the bones ①, shred or dice the meat ②, and return to kettle. Simmer broth for another 10 minutes. Skim fat off the surface ③ and serve.

Brandied Apple Soup

YIELD

4 servings

Per serving
calories 291, protein 4 g,
fat 13 g, sodium 603 mg,
carbohydrates 37 g, potassium
559 mg

TIME

30 minutes preparation
50 minutes cooking

INGREDIENTS

3 leeks
4 tart apples
1 cup cubed rutabaga
Seeds from 2 cardamom pods
¼ teaspoon coriander seeds
¼ cup butter
2 cups chicken stock
¾ cup unsweetened apple juice
2 tablespoons Apple Jack brandy

Nutmeg
Cinnamon
Salt and pepper
Lemon juice

Cut a round of wax paper to fit the top of a 5- or 6-quart pan (not iron) with a tight-fitting lid ①. Butter one side of this round. Set aside. Clean the leeks. Chop coarsely.

Peel, core, and dice 3 of the apples ②. Add the leeks, diced apples, rutabaga, cardamom and coriander seeds, and butter to the pan. Cover with wax paper, with buttered side facing the fruit and vegetables ③. Cover pan with lid and sweat the apples and vegetables for 15 minutes over low heat until the fruit and vegetables are softened. Remove and discard paper. Add the chicken stock and apple juice, cover, and simmer for 30 minutes.

Remove from heat and let stand for 20 minutes or until soup is somewhat cool. Transfer mixture into batches to a blender or food processor and purée. Return purée to the pan and add Apple Jack, a dash each of nutmeg and cinnamon, and salt and pepper to taste. Heat soup until very hot.

Core the remaining apple but do not peel. Cut in half and then into 16 slices lengthwise, as petals. Brush with lemon juice to keep from discoloring, then pour soup in bowls. Arrange 4 slices to resemble apple blossom petals in each bowl.

Papaya-Cantaloupe Soup

YIELD

4 servings

Per serving
calories 238, protein 8 g,
fat 8 g, sodium 183 mg,
carbohydrates 35 g,
potassium 1203 mg

TIME

10 minutes preparation
2 hours chilling

INGREDIENTS

1 papaya
2 medium cantaloupes
½ cup plain yogurt
½ cup kefir cheese
1 cup skim or evaporated skim milk
¼ teaspoon each ground cinnamon
    and nutmeg
Mint sprigs

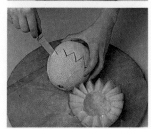

Peel ① and seed ② the papaya. Cut the cantaloupes in half and remove seeds. Scoop out almost all of the flesh. Flute edges ③.

Place yogurt, cheese, skim milk, spices, and flesh of cantaloupes into a blender or food processor. Blend until smooth and creamy, then chill. Fill melon halves with soup and garnish with mint.

LIGHT MEALS, SNACKS, AND SANDWICHES

Molded Salmon Mousse

YIELD

6 to 8 servings

Per serving (6)
calories 416, protein 23 g,
fat 34 g, sodium 634 mg,
carbohydrates 4 g,
potassium 159 mg

TIME

20 minutes preparation
3 hours chilling

INGREDIENTS

2 envelopes unflavored gelatin
1/2 cup cold water
1/3 cup lemon juice
3 cans (7 ounces each) salmon
1 cup mayonnaise
1 1/2 cups finely chopped celery
1/3 cup finely chopped green pepper
2 scallions, chopped
Salt and pepper
Lettuce leaves
Cucumber slices

In a saucepan, combine gelatin, cold water, and lemon juice. Stir over medium heat until mixture is very hot.

Drain, skin, bone, and then flake the salmon ①. In a bowl, mix salmon, mayonnaise, celery, green pepper, and scallions. Stir in gelatin mixture. Season to taste with salt and pepper.

Spray a 6-cup mold with Pam or lightly oil it ②. Pour gelatin mixture into mold ③ and chill until firm, about 3 hours.

To unmold, dip mold into lukewarm water for a few seconds, tap to loosen, and invert onto a platter. Garnish mousse with lettuce leaves and cucumber slices. Serve with herb biscuits and black olives.

Crab-Stuffed Avocado

YIELD

6 servings

Per serving
calories 340, protein 15 g,
fat 25 g, sodium 339 mg,
carbohydrates 18 g,
potassium 955 mg

TIME

10 minutes preparation
1 hour chilling

INGREDIENTS

2 cups flaked crab meat
1 cup chopped celery and leaves
½ cup sliced pitted black olives
2 tablespoons chopped chives
3 hard-cooked eggs, chopped
Sour cream, about ½ cup
Salt
3 avocados, halved and seeded
Lemon juice
3 navel oranges

In a bowl, mix crab meat, celery, olives, chives, eggs, and enough sour cream to make a moist mixture ①. Season to taste with salt.

Place avocados on serving plates and sprinkle the cut surface with lemon juice to prevent darkening ②. Fill hollows with crab mixture. Peel the oranges and divide into sections ③. Surround avocados with orange sections. Chill until ready to serve. Serve with cold borscht topped with sour cream and slices of pumpernickel bread.

Tuna Ring with Macaroni Salad

YIELD

4–6 servings

Per serving (4)
calories 608, protein 36 g,
fat 26 g, sodium 1277 mg,
carbohydrates 60 g,
potassium 1257 mg

TIME

15 minutes preparation
2–3 hours chilling

RING

2 envelopes unflavored gelatin
3½ cups tomato juice
Juice of 1 lemon
1 tablespoon Worcestershire sauce
1 small onion, grated
2 cans (7 ounces each) tuna, drained
    and flaked
1 cup minced celery

MACARONI SALAD

3 cups cooked elbow macaroni
1 cup shredded carrots
1 green pepper, chopped
1 can (1 pound, 4 ounces) pineapple
    chunks, drained
⅓ cup mayonnaise
⅓ cup sour cream

Mix gelatin and ½ cup of the juice in a small saucepan. Stir over low heat until mixture is hot. Pour into a bowl and stir in remaining tomato juice, lemon juice, and Worcestershire sauce. Chill until slightly thickened and syrupy.

Fold onion, tuna, and celery into gelatin mixture. Pour mixture into a lightly oiled 6-cup ring mold. Chill until firm.

For salad, mix macaroni with carrots, pepper, pineapple chunks, and mayonnaise and sour cream. Chill.

When ready to serve, dip mold into lukewarm water for a few seconds, run a knife around the edge, and then tap to loosen ①. Place a serving platter on top of mold ②, then invert and unmold ③. Fill center with macaroni salad. Serve with slices of Irish soda bread.

Stuffed Pasta Shells with Red and White Cole Slaw

YIELD

6 servings

Per serving
calories 498, protein 26 g,
fat 28 g, sodium 672 mg,
carbohydrates 36 g,
potassium 578 mg

TIME

15 minutes preparation
20 minutes cooking
1 hour chilling

INGREDIENTS

18 large pasta shells
1½ cups finely chopped cooked
    chicken
1½ cups finely chopped cooked ham
½ cup minced celery
1 tart apple, peeled, cored, and
    chopped
2 sweet gherkins, minced
⅓ cup mayonnaise
Juice of 1 lemon
Pinch of dry mustard
Salt

COLE SLAW

3 cups shredded red cabbage
3 cups shredded green cabbage
1 small onion, minced
⅓ cup mayonnaise
⅓ cup sour cream
1 teaspoon celery seed

Cook pasta shells in boiling salted water according to package directions. Drain and place into cold water ①.

Mix chicken, ham, celery, apple, gherkins, mayonnaise, lemon juice, and mustard ②. Season to taste with salt.

Drain shells and dry on absorbent paper. Stuff shells with salad mixture ③ and place on serving platter. Spoon extra salad around shells, and chill.

Mix ingredients for cole slaw in a bowl until well blended, then chill.

Serve shells with red and white cole slaw and slices of crusty Italian bread.

Roast Beef and Cucumbers in Horseradish Sauce

YIELD

4 servings

Per serving
calories 203, protein 22 g,
fat 10 g, sodium 273 mg,
carbohydrates 5 g,
potassium 582 mg

TIME

10 minutes preparation

INGREDIENTS

¹/₂ pound lean rare roast beef, sliced
1 medium cucumber, peeled in
   alternate strips
¹/₂ pound fresh spinach, rinsed and
   dried
¹/₂ cup kefir or neufchatel cheese
1–2 tablespoons freshly grated or
   prepared horseradish
1 tablespoon skim milk (optional)
1 teaspoon lemon juice
Salt and freshly ground pepper

Cut beef into thin julienne strips. Cut cucumber in half lengthwise ①.
Scoop out seeds with spoon ②. Thinly slice ③ and add to roast beef.

Chop spinach and set aside.

Mix remaining ingredients and fold into roast beef mixture. On a serving platter, arrange chopped fresh spinach and add roast beef salad.
Chill before serving.

Easy Pâté with Vegetables and Frittata

YIELD

6 servings

Per serving
calories 575, protein 23 g,
fat 50 g, sodium 1845 mg,
carbohydrates 9 g,
potassium 525 mg

TIME

20 minutes preparation
20–25 minutes cooking
1–2 hours chilling

INGREDIENTS

1 pound good-quality liverwurst
1 package (3 ounces) cream cheese
1/4 cup butter
1/3 cup minced pitted black olives
1 clove garlic, mashed
Assorted raw vegetables: carrots,
　zucchini, mushrooms, tomatoes,
　celery, broccoli or cauliflower
　flowerets

FRITTATA

10 eggs
1/4 cup water
2 teaspoons salt
2 tablespoons olive oil
1 green pepper, chopped
1 onion, chopped
3 tomatoes, chopped

In a bowl, mix liverwurst with cream cheese and butter until soft and fluffy ①. Fold in olives and garlic. Place into serving bowl. Chill.

Cut the vegetables into desired pieces: slice the carrots and zucchini, remove stems from mushrooms and flute caps, cut tomatoes into wedges, chunk celery, separate broccoli or cauliflower flowerets. Wrap and chill vegetables.

When ready, prepare frittata. Beat eggs with water and salt. In a large 10-inch skillet, heat olive oil and sauté the pepper and onion for 10 minutes. Add tomatoes and sauté for another 5 minutes. Add eggs ② and cook without stirring until golden brown on the bottom. Place skillet under broiler 8 inches away from source of heat ③ and broil until egg is golden and feels firm to the touch. Remove from broiler and cool. Invert frittata onto a serving platter. Serve pâté with vegetables around it. Serve frittata cold, cut into long, thin wedges. Accompany with rye toast.

Country Omelette

YIELD

3 to 4 servings

Per serving (3)
calories 695, protein 37 g,
fat 55 g, sodium 1570 mg,
carbohydrates 11 g,
potassium 721 mg

TIME

15 minutes preparation
10 minutes cooking

INGREDIENTS

2 tablespoons butter
2 teaspoons olive oil
1 slice (about ¼ pound)
   smoked ham, diced
2 Spanish sausages (chorizos) or 2
   Italian sausages, simmered 5
   minutes, then diced
1 medium potato, peeled and finely
   diced
6 eggs, lightly beaten

1 tablespoon minced fresh parsley
1 tablespoon minced scallions (white
   part only)
Salt and pepper to taste

In a skillet or omelette pan, heat 1 tablespoon butter and the olive oil; add diced ham and sausages, and sauté for about 2 minutes over medium heat until lightly browned ①. Remove ham and sausages and reserve. Add potato to pan; sauté while stirring until soft and golden brown. Combine eggs with parsley and scallions; season with salt and pepper. Stir in ham and sausages.

Pour egg mixture into the pan. Blend quickly with the potato and cook over moderate heat, shaking the pan a few times to prevent sticking. When the edge of the omelette starts to set, put the remaining butter on the edge of the omelette ② and tilt pan to let butter flow all around it ③. After about 2 minutes, put pan under a medium broiler to brown the top.

NOTE This is an open-faced omelette and should not be folded.

Goat Cheese Soufflé

YIELD

Serves 4

Per serving
calories 390, protein 12 g,
fat 27 g, sodium 481 mg,
carbohydrates 22 g,
potassium 186 mg

TIME

15 minutes preparation
35 minutes cooking

INGREDIENTS

4 tablespoons butter
3 tablespoons browned bread crumbs
2 tablespoons flour
1 cup milk
¼ pound dry goat cheese, such as
   Bucheron or Pouligny
1 heaping teaspoon Dijon-style
   mustard
Pinch of cayenne
Freshly ground black pepper to taste
4 eggs, separated
1 extra egg white

Set the oven at 400 degrees. Use 1 tablespoon of the butter to grease an 8-cup soufflé dish. Use half the bread crumbs to coat the inside of the dish ①.

Melt the remaining butter in a saucepan and whisk in the flour. Add the milk off the heat, whisking constantly until the mixture is completely smooth, then return to the heat and cook, stirring constantly, until it comes to a boil. Simmer gently for 2 minutes, then remove from the heat. Crumble the goat cheese and add it to the hot sauce (remove any rind on the cheese). Add the mustard, cayenne, black pepper, and egg yolks, 1 at a time.

Beat the 5 egg whites until they hold stiff peaks ② and stir 1 large spoonful into the hot sauce. Fold in the remaining whites as lightly as possible ③, then pour the soufflé mixture into the dish. Sprinkle the remaining bread crumbs on top and bake the soufflé for 35 minutes or until it is puffed and brown and set in the middle. Quickly tie a white linen napkin around the collar of the dish and set in on a platter. Serve at once with a large spoon.

Midwestern Deviled Eggs

YIELD

6 servings

Per serving
calories 309, protein 12 g,
fat 28 g, sodium 632 mg,
carbohydrates 3 g,
potassium 165 mg

TIME

45 minutes preparation
25 minutes cooking

INGREDIENTS

1 dozen small or medium eggs
6 tablespoons unsalted butter,
  softened
2 tablespoons mayonnaise
1 tablespoon Dijon-style mustard
1 teaspoon salt
1 teaspoon pepper

GARNISHES

1/4 cup chopped fresh parsley
1/4 cup chopped scallions, both green
  and white parts
1/4 cup crumbled bacon bits

Place eggs in a saucepan with enough water to cover by 1 inch. Cover and bring to a boil. Remove from heat and let stand 20 minutes. Cool eggs in cold water, then tap the shells against side of pan to crack. Peel eggs, and cut in half. Remove yolks to a sieve placed over a mixer bowl.

Set whites aside. Push yolks through sieve ① and, with beaters, beat in softened butter, mayonnaise, mustard, salt, and pepper ②. Taste and correct seasoning according to your palate.

Place eggs back together with some of stuffing along edges ③. Roll 4 eggs in chopped parsley, 4 eggs in chopped scallion, and 4 eggs in crumbled bacon. Wrap 2 eggs of each type for each person and serve with rolls, a slice of cold luncheon meat, and carrot sticks.

Spanish Seafood Hero

YIELD

2 servings

Per serving
calories 674, protein 28 g,
fat 23 g, sodium 517 mg,
carbohydrates 89 g,
potassium 476 mg

TIME

8 minutes preparation
2 hours marinating

INGREDIENTS

1/3 pound fresh bay scallops
3 tablespoons lime juice
1/8 teaspoon white pepper
1 scallion, minced
1 small tomato, chopped
2 black olives, sliced
1/2 hot pepper, minced (optional)
2 tablespoons olive oil
Pinch of cumin
2 hero rolls
2 lettuce leaves

Wash and drain scallops ①. Toss in shallow glass bowl with lime juice and pepper. Cover and marinate 2 hours or overnight in refrigerator.

Drain scallops, reserving juice, and toss with scallion, tomato, black olives, and red pepper.

Mix olive oil with 1 tablespoon of reserved juice. Add cumin and toss with the scallop mixture ②. Taste and correct seasonings. (This can be done ahead of time and refrigerated covered.)

Split each hero roll and pull out some of insides ③.

Place a lettuce leaf on each roll. Top with scallops. Replace top of hero. Wrap each in plastic wrap and take along an orange for dessert.

Indian Delight

YIELD

2 servings

Per serving

calories 694, protein 41 g,
fat 41 g, sodium 345 mg,
carbohydrates 40 g,
potassium 471 mg

TIME

10 minutes preparation

INGREDIENTS

1½ cups diced cooked chicken
¼ cup salted peanuts
3 scallions, sliced
¼ cup mayonnaise, approximately
¼ teaspoon curry powder
1 tablespoon chutney
2 large pita breads

Mix chicken pieces, peanuts, and scallions with mayonnaise, curry powder, and chutney ①. Blend well. Taste and correct seasoning. Split pita breads ② and stuff with chicken salad ③. Wrap securely and pack along with a banana or green seedless grapes.

Parisian Poulet

YIELD

2 servings

Per serving

calories 644, protein 51 g, fat 25 g, sodium 976 mg, carbohydrates 49 g, potassium 428 mg

TIME

15 minutes preparation

INGREDIENTS

2 shallots
1 loaf French bread
8 leaves bibb lettuce
1 large whole chicken breast, cooked
   and sliced
1 tablespoon Dijon-style mustard
4 ounces gruyère cheese, shredded

Chop the shallots ①. Split bread in half lengthwise. Pull out some of centers ②.

Place lettuce on 1 half; top with sliced chicken. Spread mustard over other half ③. Sprinkle with chopped shallots and top with shredded gruyère cheese.

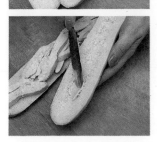

Replace top of loaf and divide in half. Wrap and serve with chilled white wine and red seedless grapes.

German Liverwurst Loaf

YIELD

2 servings

Per serving
calories 1241, protein 51 g, fat 78 g, sodium 3098 mg, carbohydrates 81 g, potassium 737 mg

TIME

30 minutes preparation
4 hours chilling

INGREDIENTS

1 pound German-style liverwurst, removed from casing
4 scallions, both green and white parts minced
2 sweet gerkins, minced
2 tablespoons minced fresh parsley
2 hard-cooked eggs, chopped
1 teaspoon mayonnaise
½ teaspoon ground coriander
1 tablespoon prepared mustard
2 hero loaves

Break up liverwurst with fork in a bowl. Add scallions, gerkins, parsley, eggs, mayonnaise, coriander, and mustard and mix well. Taste and correct seasoning.

Remove one end of the hero roll. Pull out center of bread ① and reserve for bread crumbs.

"Stuff" the liverwurst pâté into the bread, using a rubber scraper or knife ②. Replace the end and wrap in plastic wrap ③. Refrigerate to firm up.

Before wrapping for lunch, cut slices with a sharp knife and place in original shape. Wrap in aluminum foil or plastic wrap. Serve with cold beer.

New England Autumn Special

YIELD

2 servings

Per serving
calories 370, protein 23 g,
fat 8 g, sodium 448 mg,
carbohydrates 53 g,
potassium 563 mg

TIME

8 to 10 minutes
   preparation

INGREDIENTS

1 red delicious apple
Lemon juice
1 tablespoon mayonnaise
4 slices homemade bread (pumpkin,
   if you have it)
4 slices turkey breast or leftover dark
   meat
2 tablespoons cranberry relish

Slice apple ① and dip in lemon juice ② to keep from darkening.

Spread mayonnaise on bread. Top with turkey ③, apple slices, and relish. Wrap well and take along a thermos of chilled apple cider.

Scandinavian Glazed Ham Loaf

YIELD

8 servings

Per serving (loaf only)
calories 357, protein 18 g,
fat 17 g, sodium 392 mg,
carbohydrates 32 g,
potassium 351 mg

TIME

30 minutes preparation
35 minutes cooking
1 hour cooling

INGREDIENTS

³/₄ pound veal, pork, and beef, ground together
³/₄ pound boiled ham, coarsely ground
1 egg
³/₄ cup milk
1 cup soft bread crumbs
¹/₄ cup grated onion
¹/₄ cup chopped fresh parsley
¹/₂ teaspoon pepper
1 cup brown sugar
1¹/₄ teaspoons dry mustard
¹/₄ cup cider vinegar

FOR 2 SANDWICHES

1 teaspoon mustard mixed with 1 teaspoon of glaze
4 slices rye bread
2 slices ham loaf

Preheat oven to 375 degrees. Turn ground meat into large bowl. Add ground ham and, with hands or wooden spoon, mix in egg, milk, bread crumbs, onion, parsley, and pepper ①. Form into loaf and place in oiled 8¼ × 4¼-inch loaf pan ②.

Mix sugar, mustard, and vinegar in small saucepan. Bring to boil and boil 5 minutes. Pour hot glaze over ham loaf ③ and bake 30 to 35 minutes or until loaf is glazed and brown and juices run clear. Cool in pan, then refrigerate covered. This loaf can be frozen, also. It is great to serve for dinner (serves 4), then can be used the next day to make sandwiches.

To make sandwiches, spread mustard-glaze mixture on bread. Top with ham loaf slices. Wrap sandwiches and take along sweet pickles and fresh plums.

French-Bread Pizza

YIELD

4 entrees, 8 appetizers

Per serving (4)
calories 931, protein 38 g,
fat 54 g, sodium 2860 mg,
carbohydrates 74 g,
potassium 666 mg

TIME

20 minutes preparation
30 minutes cooking

INGREDIENTS

1 loaf French bread (16 inches long,
   4 inches wide)
4 tablespoons olive oil
¾ cup Tomato Sauce
1 cup chopped salami or summer
   sausage (quarter a sausage, then
   cut chunks ½ inch thick)
1 cup pimiento-stuffed green olives
1 cup grated parmesan cheese
1½ cups grated mozzarella cheese
1 green pepper, cut in strips

Preheat broiler. Cut top quarter from bread ①. Remove all but ½-inch layer of bread from inside crust ②. (Leftover bread top and insides can be used to make bread crumbs.) Brush the inside of the loaf with 2 tablespoons olive oil ③ and place under broiler until edges turn golden. Watch carefully; this only takes a minute.

Reduce the oven temperature to 350 degrees. Spread the inside of the bread with sauce. Top with salami, olives, parmesan, and mozzarella cheese. Bake for 30 minutes or until ingredients are heated through and cheeses are melted.

While bread is baking, sauté the green pepper strips in the remaining olive oil. Drain, then top baked pizza bread with sautéed peppers. Slice and serve.

FISH AND SHELLFISH

Scalloped Oysters

YIELD

4 servings

Per serving (without cheese)

calories 433, protein 14 g, fat 27 g, sodium 1202 mg, carbohydrates 32 g, potassium 233 mg

TIME

30 minutes preparation
30 minutes cooking

INGREDIENTS

1 ½ cups cracker crumbs
1 teaspoon salt
¼ teaspoon black pepper
⅓ cup butter, melted
1 pint shucked oysters, liquid reserved
    (about ½ cup)
½ cup light cream
Dash of ground mace or nutmeg
Roquefort cheese

Preheat the oven to 350 degrees.

Combine crumbs, salt, pepper, and melted butter; mix well. Layer about one-third of the crumbs in a greased 1-quart baking dish ①. Cover with half the oysters ② and oyster liquor. Add half the cream ③.

Add another third of crumbs and follow with a layer of remaining oysters, liquid, and cream. Top with remaining crumbs and sprinkle with mace. Dot generously with Roquefort cheese. Bake in hot oven until oysters are cooked and top is crisp and browned, about 30 minutes.

A Clambake on the Grill

YIELD

4 servings

Per serving
calories 543, protein 48 g,
fat 21 g, sodium 972 mg,
carbohydrates 42 g,
potassium 948 mg

TIME

45 minutes preparation
40 minutes cooking

INGREDIENTS

1 chicken, about 3 pounds, quartered
Salt and pepper
2 large onions
4 ears corn
6 dozen steamer clams or littleneck
   clams

HOT SAUCE

1 cup catsup
¼ cup horseradish
1 tablespoon lemon juice

You will need a steamer pot. The bottom holds the water about 2 inches deep and the top has a perforated bottom to allow steam to enter and cook the food. The steamer can be placed directly on the coals or on the lowest setting of the grill rack, but to make the water boil quicker, bring it to a boil in the kitchen and then place steamer on the grill.

Sprinkle chicken with salt and pepper. Cut onion into quarters ①. Place chicken into steamer along with the onions. Cover and steam for 20 minutes.

Scrub the clams and shuck the corn ②. Add to the steamer, cover, and steam for another 20 minutes, or until the clams are open.

Mix the catsup, horseradish, and lemon juice and place into a bowl for dipping clams ③. Serve with melted butter, lemon wedges, crusty bread, and cold beer.

Easy Scallop Stew

YIELD

2 to 3 servings

Per serving (3)
calories 283, protein 30 g,
fat 9 g, sodium 1358 mg,
carbohydrates 18 g, potassium
1140 mg

TIME

10 minutes preparation
20 minutes cooking

INGREDIENTS

1 pound scallops or firm white-fleshed
  nonoily fish fillets
1 1/2 tablespoons olive oil
1/3 cup chopped scallions (green and
  white parts)
2 cloves garlic, chopped
3 cups fish stock or chicken broth
1 cup diced peeled potatoes
2 teaspoons freshly grated horseradish
  or 4 teaspoons well-drained
  prepared horseradish

Juice of 1/2 lemon
1 bay leaf
1 teaspoon tamari or soy sauce
Dash of cracked red pepper
1/2 teaspoon crushed dried thyme
1/2 teaspoon dried tarragon leaves
3 tablespoons chopped fresh coriander

If large scallops are used, cut them in half ①. If using fish, cut into bite-size pieces.

Heat oil in a heavy soup kettle over medium heat and sauté the scallions until soft and transparent ②. Add garlic and sauté a few seconds. Add stock, potatoes, horseradish, lemon juice, bay leaf, tamari, cracked pepper, thyme, and tarragon and bring to a boil. Skim top, if necessary ③, then reduce to a simmer, cover and cook slowly for 10 to 12 minutes. Add the scallops or fish and cook slowly uncovered for 5 to 6 minutes, or until scallops or fish flake when tested with a fork. Remove bay leaf and garnish soup with the fresh coriander.

Scallops and Mussels Remoulade

YIELD

6 servings

Per serving
calories 439, protein 22 g,
fat 32 g, sodium 906 mg,
carbohydrates 10 g,
potassium 705 mg

TIME

25 minutes preparation
20 minutes cooking
1–2 hours chilling

INGREDIENTS

48 mussels
1 pound sea scallops
1 small onion, chopped
1 clove garlic, chopped
1 cup dry white wine
1 cup chicken broth
1 cup mayonnaise
Juice of 1 lime
1 dill pickle, minced
1 tablespoon prepared mustard

1 tablespoon finely chopped parsley
1 tablespoon finely chopped chives
Boston lettuce leaves

Scrub mussels and pull off the beards—those black stringy sections ①. Place mussels and scallops into a large saucepan. Add onion, garlic, wine, and chicken broth ②. Cover and simmer gently for 15 to 20 minutes or until mussel shells open. Drain and cool. (Broth may be used chilled as a flavorful first course, topped with lime slices.)

Remove mussels from shells ③ and place into a bowl along with scallops. Mix remaining ingredients except lettuce leaves and add to seafood. Blend thoroughly, then chill.

Serve spooned onto lettuce leaves. If desired, sprinkle with paprika, additional parsley, or chives. Serve with marinated asparagus spears and sliced tomatoes.

Herbed Mussel Soup

YIELD

6 servings

Per serving (6)
calories 668, protein 26 g,
fat 36 g, sodium 1202 mg,
carbohydrates 51 g, potassium
532 mg

TIME

20 minutes preparation
20 minutes cooking

INGREDIENTS

5 pounds mussels
1 cup butter
½ cup chopped scallions (green and
    white parts)
½ cup chopped shallots
⅓ cup finely chopped fresh parsley
3 tablespoons finely chopped chervil,
    or 1½ tablespoons crumbled dried
1 small sprig fresh tarragon, or ⅛
    teaspoon crumbled dried

1 cup cold water
1 cup dry white wine or vermouth
Freshly ground black pepper
Salt
3 small loaves Italian bread
2 cloves garlic, split
½ cup freshly grated romano or
    parmesan cheese

Preheat oven to 425 degrees. Clean mussels, discarding their fiberlike beards ①. Scrub with cold water using a stiff brush or plastic or metal soapless pad ②. Rinse in several changes of water, then drain well and set aside.

In a heavy 8-quart kettle, melt half the butter over moderate heat. Add the scallions, shallots, parsley, chervil, and tarragon. Cook, stirring often, until scallions and shallots soften and become transparent; do not brown.

Stir in water and wine or vermouth and several grindings of black pepper, along with a dash or 2 of salt. Add the mussels and cover tightly. Bring to a boil over high heat, reduce to simmer, and shake kettle once or twice up and down during the cooking process to make sure the mussels are cooking evenly. Cook for 5 to 10 minutes or until all mussels open. Discard any that do not.

While mussels are cooking, split the breads in half lengthwise. Rub each half with a piece of garlic ③, then discard garlic. Melt the remaining butter and brush over the cut sides of the bread. Top with the cheese and put in the oven for 5 to 10 minutes until browned and bubbly.

With a slotted spoon, transfer the mussels to bowls or a tureen. Strain the soup through a sieve covered with a double layer of cheesecloth directly into the bowls or tureen, pressing down with a spoon to remove all the liquid from the vegetables and herbs. Serve with the toasted cheese breads.

Shrimp Bilbaina

YIELD

4 servings

Per serving
*calories 404, protein 50 g,
fat 18 g, sodium 565 mg,
carbohydrates 6 g,
potassium 689 mg*

TIME

15 minutes preparation
5 minutes cooking

INGREDIENTS

2 dozen jumbo shrimp
3 tablespoons olive oil
2 tablespoons butter
1 large clove garlic, crushed
2 anchovy fillets, mashed
1 tablespoon tomato paste
1 teaspoon lemon juice
⅓ cup dry white wine
1 tablespoon minced fresh parsley
Salt and pepper to taste

Shell ① and devein shrimp ②. In a skillet, heat oil and butter. Sauté shrimp over moderately high heat for about 2 to 3 minutes, until they turn pink. Turn them once during cooking. Do not overcook. Remove shrimp from skillet and keep warm.

Add all other ingredients to skillet. Blend well and cook over high heat while stirring ③ for about 2 minutes, until sauce is smooth and reduced by about half. Place shrimp on a serving dish, spoon sauce over, and serve.

Shrimp, Cantonese Style

YIELD

4 to 6 servings

Per serving (4)
calories 299, protein 22 g,
fat 18 g, sodium 664 mg,
carbohydrates 11 g,
potassium 350 mg

TIME

20 to 25 minutes
preparation
6 to 8 minutes cooking

INGREDIENTS

1 pound medium shrimp
1 tablespoon cornstarch
3 cloves garlic
1 tablespoon salted black beans
3 tablespoons oil
6 slices gingerroot, 1/4 inch thick
1/4 pound ground pork or beef
3 scallions, in 1-inch pieces
1 medium egg, beaten

SAUCE A

1 tablespoon dry sherry
1 tablespoon thin soy sauce
1/2 teaspoon sugar

SAUCE B

1 1/4 tablespoons cornstarch
3/4 cup chicken broth

Peel the shrimp ①. Make a deep incision along the back; remove and discard the vein ②. Rinse thoroughly, pat dry, and coat with cornstarch. Peel and smash the garlic. Rinse the black beans under hot water, then drain well. In separate bowls, combine the sherry, soy sauce, and sugar and the cornstarch and chicken broth.

Cook the shrimp in boiling salted (1 teaspoon) water for 30 to 40 seconds. Drain and pat dry. Place on the work platter.

Heat a wok and add the oil. Heat for 15 seconds, then add the ginger slices. Stir until lightly browned, then add the garlic. Stir until lightly browned. Remove and discard both.

Add the salted beans, stir for 10 seconds, then add the ground pork. Stir vigorously to mix and break up the pork granules. Cook until the pork is no longer pink, then add the scallion pieces. Stir another 30 seconds, add the shrimp, and stir to mix well.

Mix Sauce A and pour down the sides of the wok, stirring all the while. Shovel the contents of the wok to one side. Mix Sauce B and pour down the vacated side of the wok. Stir to thicken with the point of the spatula. Mix with the shrimp ③.

Reduce the heat. Pour the beaten egg over the shrimp. Allow to set for 15 seconds, then fold in slowly until soft threads appear. Stir gently to mix. Remove to a platter and serve immediately.

Deep-Fried Crispy Shrimp

YIELD

4 to 6 servings

Per serving (4)
(with Sauce A)

calories 610, protein 19 g,
fat 40 g, sodium 1455 mg,
carbohydrates 42 g,
potassium 354 mg

TIME

30 minutes preparation
12 to 15 minutes cooking

INGREDIENTS

1 pound medium shrimp in their shells
½ head iceberg lettuce
8 cups oil

BATTER

1½ cups all-purpose flour
1 tablespoon baking powder
1 teaspoon salt
½ cup oil
1–1¼ cups cold water

SAUCE A

1½ tablespoons thin soy sauce
3 tablespoons mild vinegar
2 tablespoons shredded gingerroot
1 tablespoon oriental sesame oil

SAUCE B

2 tablespoons hoisin sauce
1 tablespoon tomato catsup
1 teaspoon chili sauce (Red Devil or
   the like)
1 teaspoon dry sherry
1 tablespoon minced scallion

Remove the shells from the shrimp but leave the last segment and the tails. Split the shrimp down the back until almost completely open ①. Remove the vein. Place the shrimp in a bowl of ice water.

Combine the dry ingredients for the batter. Mix well, then add the oil a little at a time until oil and flour are thoroughly mixed; break up any large lumps. Now add the water a little at a time ②, stirring constantly in one direction. Eventually, the batter will become smooth and silky. Stop adding water when you attain the consistency of a thin pancake batter. Allow the batter to rest, covered, for at least 15 minutes.

Prepare sauce A, B, or both. Shred the lettuce and place on a platter. Cover with clear wrap until ready for use.

Place the oil in a wok and heat to 375 degrees. While the oil is heating, drain the shrimp, pat dry, and dip in the batter, leaving the tails exposed for easy handling. Line a work platter with paper toweling.

Place 8 to 10 shrimp in the hot oil and cook until the batter turns a golden brown. Remove with a large strainer to the work platter ③. Do the remaining shrimp in the same manner, making sure that the oil reaches 375 degrees before adding the shrimp.

Remove the covering from the lettuce. Place the sauce bowl(s) in the center. Place the shrimp, tails up, around the perimeter of the platter. Serve immediately.

VARIATION *For additional color, garnish with lemon and tomato wedges.*

Fruited Tofu-Shrimp Sauté

YIELD

4 servings

Per serving
calories 198, protein 23 g,
fat 7 g, sodium 130 mg,
carbohydrates 11 g,
potassium 327 mg

TIME

5 minutes preparation
6 minutes cooking

INGREDIENTS

1 teaspoon each butter and safflower oil
2 cloves garlic, minced or crushed
²/₃ pound shelled medium shrimp,
    cleaned and deveined
1 pound tofu, cut in 1-inch cubes
½ cup each red and green seedless
    grapes
¼ cup lemon juice
¼ cup minced fresh parsley
4 lemon wheels for garnish

In a large nonstick skillet, heat butter and oil over medium heat. Add garlic, shrimp, and tofu; sauté until shrimp just begin to turn pink, about 4 minutes ①.

Push food in skillet to edges of pan and warm grapes briefly in center ②. All at once, add lemon juice and parsley. Swirl pan to distribute juices and gently mix fruit with seafood.

Transfer mixture to a warmed serving platter or individual dishes and garnish with lemon wheels if desired ③.

Spicy Oriental Noodles with Shrimp

YIELD

6 servings

Per serving
calories 635, protein 22 g,
fat 46 g, sodium 1306 mg,
carbohydrates 36 g,
potassium 398 mg

TIME

25 minutes preparation
15 minutes cooking
2 hours chilling

INGREDIENTS

1 pound raw shrimp
½ pound thin spaghetti or transparent
   noodles
2 cups diced tofu
1 cup peanut or sesame oil
⅓ cup red wine vinegar
½ teaspoon red pepper flakes
2 tablespoons smooth peanut butter
⅓ cup Japanese soy sauce
1 clove garlic, mashed
⅓ cup finely chopped salted peanuts
6 scallions, trimmed and sliced

Cook, shell, and devein shrimp. Wrap and chill.

Cook noodles in boiling salted water until tender, then drain and pour into a bowl ①. Add tofu and shrimp ②.

In a bowl, beat oil with vinegar, red pepper flakes, peanut butter, soy sauce, and garlic until well blended and thick ③.

Pour sauce over noodles and toss to coat all particles. Cover and chill for 1 to 2 hours. When ready to serve, toss noodles again and sprinkle with peanuts and scallions. Serve with snow peas.

Deviled Crab

YIELD

4 servings

Per serving
calories 220, protein 24 g,
fat 10 g, sodium 1399 mg,
carbohydrates 6 g,
potassium 251 mg

TIME

30 minutes preparation
10 minutes cooking

INGREDIENTS

1 tablespoon butter
1½ tablespoons cracker crumbs
¾ cup milk
2 eggs
¼ teaspoon salt
1 teaspoon prepared mustard
¼ teaspoon cayenne
3 tablespoons finely chopped green
    pepper
¼ teaspoon Tabasco
1 pound fresh, frozen, or canned
    crabmeat, picked over

Preheat the oven to 400 degrees.

Melt butter in saucepan; add crumbs and milk and blend well ①. Boil until thick, then remove from heat. Beat together the eggs, salt, mustard, and cayenne, then add to milk mixture ②. Add green pepper, Tabasco, and crab and stir well.

Spoon mixture into 8 buttered crab shells or baking dishes ③, rounding tops. Brown in hot oven for about 10 minutes. If desired, run shells or baking dishes under broiler to brown tops.

Maine Lobster Stew

YIELD

4 servings

Per serving
calories 274, protein 17 g,
fat 19 g, sodium 330 mg,
carbohydrates 9 g,
potassium 392 mg

TIME

10 minutes preparation
15 minutes cooking
2 hours chilling

INGREDIENTS

4 tablespoons butter
1 cup cooked lobster meat
2 cups milk
½ cup light cream or evaporated milk
Sprinkle of paprika
Freshly ground black pepper

Melt 3 tablespoons butter in a heavy saucepan and add lobster meat. Simmer until both lobster and butter turn very red ①, about 2 to 3 minutes.

Add milk and cream ②. Heat almost to boiling but do not boil. Chill for at least 2 hours.

Reheat stew in a double boiler ③. Sprinkle with paprika, and add remaining butter and pepper. Serve with oyster crackers and pickles.

Crêpes with Lobster-Mushroom Filling

YIELD

6 servings

Per serving
calories 460, protein 26 g, fat 28 g, sodium 775 mg, carbohydrates 26 g, potassium 504 mg

TIME

25 minutes preparation
45 minutes cooking
1 hour chilling

CRÊPES

1 cup all-purpose flour
1½ cups milk
2 eggs
1 tablespoon butter, melted
¼ teaspoon salt

FILLING

4 tablespoons butter or margarine
2 cups sliced fresh mushrooms
3 cups cooked lobster, cut into bite-size pieces

½ teaspoon salt
¼ teaspoon pepper
¼ teaspoon paprika
Dash of cayenne
2 cups half-and-half
½ cup dry sherry
3 egg yolks
2 tablespoons grated parmesan cheese
2 tablespoons grated swiss cheese

To make crêpes, place flour, milk, eggs, melted butter, and salt in a blender and process until smooth. Refrigerate for a minimum of 1 hour.

Heat a 7-inch frying pan and coat lightly with butter. Measure 2 tablespoons batter into pan ① and swirl it around quickly ②. Cook for 45 seconds and turn ③. Cook for 15 seconds on second side. Turn pan over and let crêpe drop onto wax paper. Repeat until all crêpes are made.

In a large skillet heat butter and sauté mushrooms; add lobster meat, salt, pepper, paprika, and cayenne. Mix well.

In a saucepan heat half-and-half to scalding, then add sherry. Beat egg yolks with a wire whisk. Beat a small amount of the half-and-half into the egg yolks and return to pan. Cook, over low heat, until slightly thickened. Do not boil.

Pour sauce over lobster/mushroom mixture and mix thoroughly.

Preheat oven to 350 degrees. Spread about ½ cup filling down center of each crêpe. Fold sides over and place, seam side down, in shallow pan. Pour any remaining sauce over crêpes. Combine parmesan and swiss cheese and sprinkle over crêpes. Place in oven for 20 minutes or until filling is hot and cheeses are melted.

Italian Stuffed Lobster with Artichokes

YIELD

4 servings

Per serving
calories 976, protein 56 g,
fat 80 g, sodium 990 mg,
carbohydrates 15 g,
potassium 1049 mg

TIME

30 minutes preparation
40 minutes cooking
1–2 hours chilling

INGREDIENTS

4 lobsters, each weighing 1½ pounds
4 artichokes
1 cup (4 ounces) diced mozzarella
  cheese
4 plum tomatoes, diced
3 egg yolks
3 cloves garlic
1 tablespoon lemon juice
½ teaspoon salt
¼ teaspoon pepper

1 cup olive oil
¼ cup chicken broth
4 anchovy fillets
½ cup toasted pine nuts
8 pitted black olives, sliced

Drop lobsters into boiling salted water. When water reboils, boil for 5 minutes, then drain and cool.

Trim stems and tips of leaves on artichokes ①, and cook in boiling salted water until easily pierced, about 30 to 35 minutes. Drain, cool, and then chill.

With a sharp knife, cut lobsters in half and open out ②. Remove meat from body and claws ③. Dice meat and mix with mozzarella cheese and tomatoes. Stuff mixture back into body shells. Chill.

Combine egg yolks, garlic, lemon juice, salt, and pepper in a blender. Whirl until smooth. With motor running, slowly add oil drop by drop until all oil is added. Slowly drip in chicken broth. Add anchovy fillets and blend until smooth. Chill.

When ready to serve, thin dressing, if necessary, to a heavy cream consistency using extra chicken broth. Drizzle some of the dressing over lobster salad. Sprinkle with pine nuts and olives. Place remaining dressing into small bowls and use for dipping artichoke leaves. This is good accompanied by sesame seed breadsticks.

Shrimp, Clam, and Mussel Paella

YIELD

6 servings

Per serving
calories 431, protein 28 g,
fat 12 g, sodium 938 mg,
carbohydrates 50 g,
potassium 609 mg

TIME

10 minutes preparation
40 minutes cooking

INGREDIENTS

¼ cup olive oil
1 large onion, chopped
2 cloves garlic, chopped
1½ cups rice, uncooked
⅛ teaspoon saffron
1 bottle (8 ounces) clam juice
3 cups chicken broth, canned or
   homemade (approximately)
1 bay leaf
1 pound shrimp, shelled and deveined
18 littleneck clams, scrubbed well

18 mussels, scrubbed well
1 cup peas, fresh or frozen
2 tablespoons chopped pimiento
Salt and pepper

In a large skillet, heat oil and sauté onion and garlic until soft. Add rice and saffron and cook 5 minutes, stirring constantly ①. Add clam juice, 2 cups chicken broth, and bay leaf to skillet and simmer, covered, for 10 minutes.

Remove cover, stir in 1 additional cup chicken broth and shrimp. Cover and cook 5 minutes. Remove cover and add additional chicken broth if rice is dry.

Add clams and mussels to rice mixture and poke them into the rice ②. Cover and cook 10 minutes or until they open; discard any that do not open. Add peas and pimiento ③. Season with salt and pepper. Reheat and serve.

Grill-Baked Sea Bass

YIELD

4 servings

Per serving
calories 315, protein 36 g,
fat 17 g, sodium 355 mg,
carbohydrates 4 g,
potassium 788 mg

TIME

15 minutes preparation
40 minutes grilling

INGREDIENTS

4 pound sea bass, scaled and cleaned
1/3 cup melted butter or margarine
Juice of 1 lemon or lime
1/2 cup coarsely chopped fresh dill
Salt, paprika, garlic powder, onion
    powder

Wash fish and pat dry.

Brush some of the butter on a piece of heavy-duty foil large enough to hold fish ①. Place fish on foil and brush with remaining butter and lemon juice ②. Sprinkle evenly with dill, salt, paprika, garlic powder and onion powder ③.

Seal foil into a packet and place 8 inches above gray coals. Grill for 35 to 40 minutes, turning packet every 10 minutes. Serve with lemon wedges, foil-baked new potatoes and sliced onions, stir-fried mushrooms, and peas.

NOTE Other fish that can be used for this recipe include black bass, red snapper, striped bass.

Trout in Parchment Paper

YIELD

6 servings

Per serving
calories 280, protein 36 g, fat 13 g, sodium 204 mg, carbohydrates 5 g, potassium 751 mg

TIME

15 minutes preparation
25 minutes cooking

INGREDIENTS

2 tablespoons butter or margarine
3 scallions, minced
1 carrot, grated
1 clove garlic, minced
1 cup chopped fresh mushrooms
2 tablespoons chopped fresh Italian (flat) parsley
6 trout, about 8 ounces each
3 small zucchini, thinly sliced
Salt and pepper
½ teaspoon oregano

2 tablespoons lemon juice
2 tablespoons olive oil
1 lemon, thinly sliced

Preheat oven to 400 degrees. In a medium skillet melt butter and sauté scallions, carrot, and garlic for 3 minutes. Add mushrooms and parsley and cook another 2 minutes.

Wash trout and pat dry with paper toweling.

Divide sautéed vegetables into 6 equal portions and place 1 portion in cavity of each trout.

Place each trout on an oiled 12 by 15-inch piece of parchment paper or aluminum foil. Slide a few slices of zucchini under the trout and place a few on top.

Combine salt, pepper, oregano, and lemon juice and sprinkle it over the fish. Place a thin slice of lemon on each trout ①.

Bring up the 12-inch sides of the parchment and fold, drug store style ②. Fold edges of sides under with several folds ③. Place on a baking sheet and bake in hot oven for 15 to 20 minutes.

Fried Smelts

YIELD

6 servings

Per serving
calories 329, protein 19 g,
fat 22 g, sodium 481 mg,
carbohydrates 13 g,
potassium 451 mg

TIME

15 minutes preparation
15 minutes cooking

INGREDIENTS

1 pound smelts or other small fish
1 can (2 ounces) anchovy fillets
1/2 cup all-purpose flour
1/4 teaspoon salt
1/8 teaspoon pepper
3 tablespoons butter or margarine
3 tablespoons vegetable oil
Lemon slices and dill sprigs for garnish

SAUCE

2 tablespoons minced onion
1 1/2 tablespoons all-purpose flour
1/2 teaspoon salt
1 1/4 cups half-and-half
1 egg yolk, beaten
1 tablespoon lemon juice
1 tablespoon chopped fresh dill

Remove heads and clean fish ①. Drain anchovies, reserving oil. Cut anchovies in half lengthwise and place one half anchovy inside each fish ②.

Combine flour with salt and pepper and roll each fish in it ③. Set aside.

To make sauce, heat reserved anchovy oil in a small saucepan. Add the minced onion and cook until tender, about 3 minutes. Blend in flour and salt. Gradually stir in half-and-half. Cook, stirring constantly, until thickened.

Add a little of the hot sauce to the egg yolk and return mixture to pot. Heat until thickened, stirring constantly. Add lemon juice and dill.

In a large skillet, melt butter and oil. Add fish, a few at a time, and cook until crisp, about 5 minutes.

Spoon sauce over fish, and serve on cooked rice. Garnish with lemon and dill.

Fish Teriyaki

YIELD

4 servings

Per serving
*calories 487, protein 44 g,
fat 28 g, sodium 1498 mg,
carbohydrates 4 g,
potassium 1046 mg*

TIME

5 minutes preparation
20 minutes marinating
20 minutes cooking

INGREDIENTS

4 tablespoons Japanese soy sauce
4 tablespoons mirin (see note)
4 tablespoons sake or dry sherry
1 clove garlic, crushed
1 teaspoon grated gingerroot
4 pieces mackerel fillet, or tuna or
    bluefish (about 2 pounds total)

Place all ingredients except fish in a saucepan. Bring to a boil and simmer for 1 minute. Remove from heat and allow to cool.

Place mixture in a bowl, add fish, stir to coat well ①, and marinate for 20 minutes. Drain fish and reserve marinade.

Preheat the broiler. Place fish in the broiler pan ②, and grill for about 5 minutes per side, depending on the thickness of the pieces. Brush 4 or 5 times during broiling with reserved marinade ③. When cooked, the fish should have a deep brown, shiny glaze.

NOTE *Mirin is a sweet cooking rice wine, available in many supermarkets on their oriental food shelves and in all oriental food stores. If mirin is not available, add more dry sherry to the marinade and also add 1 tablespoon sugar.*

Crab-Stuffed Fillets on Spinach Noodles

YIELD

6 servings

Per serving
calories 449, protein 42 g,
fat 21 g, sodium 768 mg,
carbohydrates 21 g,
potassium 880 mg

TIME

35 minutes preparation
40 minutes cooking

INGREDIENTS

8 ounces crab meat, fresh or frozen
1/2 cup finely chopped celery
2 tablespoons butter or margarine
1/4 cup chopped scallions
2 tablespoons chopped Italian (flat) parsley
1 tablespoon lemon juice
1/4 teaspoon salt
1/8 teaspoon black pepper
1/4 teaspoon dill weed
6 fillets
Salt and pepper
2 cups spinach noodles, cooked and drained

2 tablespoons grated parmesan cheese

SAUCE

3 tablespoons butter or margarine
2 tablespoons all-purpose flour
1/2 teaspoon salt
1/8 teaspoon pepper
1 cup half-and-half
1 1/4 cups milk
2 egg yolks, beaten
2 tablespoons dry sherry

Pick over crab and remove any cartilage.

Sauté celery in butter; add crab and scallions, parsley, lemon juice, salt, pepper, and dill weed. Place a spoonful of crab stuffing on each fillet and spread into an even layer ①. Starting at the narrow end, roll up fillets ② and fasten with toothpicks ③.

To make the sauce, melt the butter and blend in flour, salt, and pepper. Add half-and-half and milk. Cook, stirring constantly until thickened and smooth. Add a small amount of the sauce to the egg yolks and return to sauce. Stir in sherry; cook over low heat 2 to 3 minutes.

Preheat oven to 350 degrees. Combine spinach noodles with 1 1/2 cups sauce and grated parmesan cheese. Place in a buttered casserole and top with stuffed fish fillets. Cover and bake in oven for 30 minutes. Serve remaining sauce over fillets.

NOTE For the fillets, use sole, flounder, scrod, or any other firm-fleshed fish.

Fish Fillets with Creole Sauce

YIELD

4 servings

Per serving
calories 472, protein 23 g,
fat 35 g, sodium 511 mg,
carbohydrates 13 g,
potassium 858 mg

TIME

15 minutes preparation
2 hours marinating
50 minutes cooking

INGREDIENTS

1 pound fish fillets
⅓ cup olive oil
⅓ cup dry white wine
2 tablespoons lemon juice
1 clove garlic, minced
1 teaspoon dried tarragon
½ teaspoon black pepper

CREOLE SAUCE

¼ cup olive oil
⅓ cup chopped green pepper
⅓ cup chopped onion

1 clove garlic, chopped
3 large ripe tomatoes, peeled, seeded,
   and chopped
¼ cup dry red wine
3 tablespoons tomato paste
1 tablespoon chopped green chili
1 teaspoon dried tarragon
½ teaspoon salt
¼ teaspoon black pepper
¼ cup sliced black olives
Hot cooked rice

Place fish in a shallow glass dish. Combine olive oil, wine, lemon juice, garlic, tarragon, and pepper; pour over fish ① and marinate for at least 2 hours in refrigerator. Drain, discarding marinade.

In a large, deep skillet heat olive oil and sauté green pepper, onion, and garlic ②. Add tomatoes, wine, tomato paste, green chili, tarragon, salt, and pepper. Bring to a boil and cook, stirring occasionally, 5 mintues ③. Lower heat, cover, and simmer 25 minutes.

Add fish fillets and olives to sauce. Cover and poach 15 minutes or until fish is opaque and flakes easily with fork. Serve with rice.

NOTE For this recipe, use haddock, cod, tile fish, or bass fillets.

Spinach-Stuffed Fillets with Shrimp Sauce

YIELD

6 servings

Per serving
calories 352, protein 35 g,
fat 21 g, sodium 526 mg,
carbohydrates 5 g,
potassium 765 mg

TIME

40 minutes preparation
25 minutes cooking

INGREDIENTS

2 pounds fish fillets
1 package (10 ounces) frozen
   spinach, defrosted and drained
1/2 cup heavy cream
Salt and pepper
Dash of nutmeg
1/2 cup chicken broth

1/2 cup clam juice or white wine
6 ounces cooked shrimp
6 tablespoons butter
2 tablespoons all-purpose flour
2 tablespoons lemon juice

Preheat oven to 400 degrees. Wash fillets and pat dry. Combine spinach, 1 table-spoon heavy cream, salt, pepper, and nutmeg.

Lay fillets on a flat surface. Divide spinach mixture equally among them, spreading the mixture down the center of each fillet ①. Roll fillets up, pressing edges together so that the spinach cannot seep through ②.

Place fillets, seam side down, in a buttered baking pan. Pour in chicken broth and clam juice or white wine ③. Cover with a sheet of lightly buttered wax paper and poach in hot oven for 10 minutes.

Remove pan from oven and carefully poor off poaching liquid. If necessary, add more chicken broth or clam juice to make 1 cup. Set aside. (Fish can be prepared up to this point and refrigerated.)

Purée all but 3 shrimp in food processor by quickly switching it on and off 3 or 4 times, or chop it with a knife. Melt 4 tablespoons butter. With machine on, slowly pour in melted butter. Do not overprocess. If using knife, transfer shrimp to bowl and stir vigorously with fork to incorporate them.

Set oven to 350 degrees. In a small saucepan, melt remaining 2 tablespoons butter. Blend in flour, salt, and pepper to taste. Cook 2 minutes, stirring constantly.

Slowly add reserved poaching liquid and remaining heavy cream. Cook until slightly thickened, stirring constantly. Stir in lemon juice and shrimp-butter mixture.

Pour sauce over fish rolls. Cut remaining shrimp in half lengthwise and use as garnish for fish rolls. Bake in oven for 10 minutes, then serve.

NOTE *Use fillets from a small fish, such as flounder, sole, or blackfish.*

Fish Fillets with Mustard-Caper Sauce

YIELD

6 servings

Per serving
calories 231, protein 26 g,
fat 9 g, sodium 275 mg,
carbohydrates 4 g,
potassium 567 mg

TIME

5 minutes preparation
15 minutes cooking

INGREDIENTS

2 pounds fish fillets
1 cup dry white wine
2 tablespoons capers, rinsed and
   drained
1 tablespoon dijon-style mustard
½ cup heavy cream
1½ tablespoons cornstarch
2 tablespoons water

Preheat oven to 400 degrees. Wash fillets and pat dry. Arrange in buttered baking dish. Pour wine over fillets. Cut a piece of parchment
paper to fit pan. Lightly butter the paper and cover fish with it.

Bake fish in hot oven for 10 minutes. Remove pan from oven. Carefully remove poaching liquid and pour into a small saucepan ①. (Fish
can be prepared up to this point and refrigerated.)

Set oven to 350 degrees. Add capers and mustard to poaching liquid.
Bring to a boil, lower heat, and simmer for 1 minute.

Stir heavy cream into mustard mixture. Combine cornstarch with
water ② and slowly add to the sauce ③. Cook until slightly thickened.

Spoon sauce over fish and bake in oven for 10 minutes.

NOTE Use flounder, sole, striped bass, or bluefish fillets.

Poached Haddock in Tomato Sauce

YIELD

Serves 4

Per serving
calories 389, protein 44 g,
fat 14 g, sodium 382 mg,
carbohydrates 14 g,
potassium 1197 mg

TIME

10 minutes preparation
15 minutes cooking

INGREDIENTS

4 haddock steaks or fillets, each ½
  pound (or use cod or perch)
¼ cup olive oil
2 onions, chopped
2 medium carrots, thinly sliced
1 can (1 pound) Italian-style plum
  tomatoes
1 clove garlic, crushed
½ cup white wine

Salt and freshly ground black pepper
  to taste
Small handful of fresh parsley sprigs,
  finely chopped

Leave the fish at room temperature while you prepare the sauce.

Heat the oil in a large skillet that has a tight-fitting lid. Cook the on-ions over a low heat for 2 minutes or until they are soft but not brown ①. Add the carrots, cover the pan, and continue cooking 2 minutes, stirring occasionally.

Crush the tomatoes in your hand as they are added to the pan ② and add the garlic, wine, and plenty of salt and pepper to taste. Bring to a boil and leave this sauce to bubble gently for 3 minutes, uncovered.

Set the fish into the sauce and spoon some of it on top ③. Turn the heat up so the liquid comes to a boil, then lower it, cover the pan, and let the fish cook gently for 10 minutes or until it is firm to the touch and white in color.

Serve in deep plates, sprinkling each portion with chopped parsley. Pass rice pilaf or small boiled potatoes separately.

Poached Fish Pieces with Chinese Vegetables

YIELD

4 to 6 servings

Per serving (4)
calories 362, protein 27 g,
fat 20 g, sodium 873 mg,
carbohydrates 15 g,
potassium 780 mg

TIME

8 to 10 minutes
  preparation
15 to 20 minutes cooking

INGREDIENTS

1 pound firm-fleshed fish fillets
½ teaspoon salt
Pinch of sugar
1 egg white
Cornstarch to coat
3 stalks bok choy with leaves
1 can (10 ounces) straw mushrooms,
  drained
12 snow peas
4 waterchestnuts
3 cloves garlic
Dry sherry

6 cups oil
1 egg white, beaten
2 teaspoons sesame oil

SAUCE

1 cup chicken broth
1 tablespoon gin
2 tablespoons sweet vermouth
½ teaspoon salt (if necessary)
Freshly ground pepper
2 tablespoons cornstarch

Cut the fillets in half lengthwise, then on the bias into 1¼-inch pieces ①. Place in a bowl. Add salt and sugar and mix gently with fingers. Lightly beat the egg white, add to bowl, and mix gently. Coat fish with cornstarch; mix and reserve.

Split bok choy down the middle. Cut on the bias into 1-inch pieces ②; include some leaf for color. Trim the snow peas. Cut waterchestnuts into thin slices. Peel and slice garlic; moisten with dry sherry.

Combine broth, gin, wine, salt, and pepper for sauce. Remove ¼ cup and mix with the 2 tablespoons of cornstarch.

Heat oil in a wok to 250 degrees. Add fish, stir gently with a slotted spoon to loosen pieces ③, and cook for 1 minute. Remove with large strainer to a platter.

Strain the oil into a heatproof bowl. Reheat wok and add 3 tablespoons of the oil. Reduce heat and add garlic. Stir 30 seconds, turn up heat, and add vegetables. Stir for 30 seconds, then remove to platter.

Add the sauce to wok. Bring to a boil, then thicken to the desired consistency with the cornstarch mixture, adding slowly and stirring continuously. Reduce heat source, pour beaten egg white on top. Let set for 10 seconds. Fold slowly until soft white threads appear. Add fish, vegetables, and sesame oil and stir to mix. Place on serving platter and serve immediately.

VARIATION Substitute sliced fresh mushrooms for the straw mushrooms; add with the garlic.

East Indian Fish, Shrimp, and Pineapple Soup

YIELD

6 servings

Per serving
calories 368, protein 38 g,
fat 10 g, sodium 191 mg,
carbohydrates 29 g, potassium
886 mg

TIME

20 minutes preparation
45 minutes cooking

INGREDIENTS

1 package (3¾ ounces) cellophane
   noodles, or ¼ pound rice noodles
   or vermicelli
2½ pounds fresh whitefish (sole,
   snapper, flounder, perch, bass)
   or a mixture of these
½ pound fresh shrimp (about 12)
1 fresh pineapple
2½ quarts water
1 onion

8 whole black peppercorns
2 small bay leaves
¼ cup coarsely chopped celery leaves
2 sprigs fresh coriander
1 tablespoon fresh gingerroot, minced
   or 1 teaspoon ground
1 teaspoon turmeric
3–4 tablespoons vegetable oil
¼ cup scallions (green and white
   parts), finely chopped

In a bowl, soak cellophane noodles in 2 cups water for 30 minutes. (Skip if using other noodles.) Have fish cleaned and filleted, but save trimmings. Shell shrimp; with paring knife, lift out black vein. Rinse and pat dry. Set aside.

Cut crown off pineapple. Cut lengthwise through pineapple ①. Slice again into quarters ②. Cut about ¼ inch from skin and loosen fruit completely from all 4 quarters ③. Remove eyes and cut into 12 strips. Set aside.

Place fish trimmings and shrimp shells in an 8-quart saucepan and add remaining water, onion, peppercorns, bay, celery, coriander, and ginger. Bring to boil. Skim top, if necessary, then reduce heat and simmer uncovered for 25 minutes. Strain broth through a fine sieve lined with cheesecloth, pressing down hard with back of a spoon to get all the juices. Return broth to saucepan.

Drain noodles and discard water. Cut noodles into 2-inch pieces. If rice noodles or vermicelli are used, break into 2-inch pieces. Add turmeric and noodles to broth. Bring to boil, reduce heat to low, and add fish. Cover and simmer gently for 10 to 12 minutes or until fish flakes easily when tested with a fork. Add shrimp and cook 2 to 3 minutes until pink and firm. Remove bay leaf. Turn off heat and cover pot.

Heat oil in skillet and quickly sauté pineapple on both sides until lightly brown. Place fish in shallow soup dishes. Put pineapple sticks, 2 to a dish, on either side of fish. Add 2 shrimp to other side. Ladle soup over fish; garnish with scallions.

Baked Codfish

YIELD

4 servings

Per serving
calories 308, protein 41 g,
fat 11 g, sodium 354 mg,
carbohydrates 9 g,
potassium 1170 mg

TIME

15 minutes preparation
25 minutes cooking

INGREDIENTS

4 codfish or halibut steaks, about 2
   pounds total
Salt and pepper to taste
3 tablespoons olive oil
1 medium onion, minced
1 large clove garlic, crushed
½ teaspoon dried leaf thyme
1 small bay leaf
1½ cups drained and chopped
   canned tomatoes

1 tablespoon minced fresh parsley
¼ teaspoon Tabasco
1 cup dry white wine

Wipe steaks with a damp cloth. Place in 1 layer in a buttered shallow baking dish ①. Set aside.

In a skillet, heat oil and sauté onion for 2 or 3 minutes until light golden ②. Add garlic and thyme, and sauté for another minute. Add tomatoes, stir well, and simmer for 2 minutes, then add the parsley, Tabasco, and wine. Mix, then simmer for 10 minutes until sauce has slightly thickened.

Preheat oven to 400 degrees.

Remove sauce from heat, and pour through a fine-meshed strainer ③. Spoon over fish in pan. Bake in hot oven for about 10 minutes, until fish is flaky and cooked.

Herbed Salmon Steaks

YIELD

Serves 6

Per serving
calories 537, protein 46 g,
fat 34 g, sodium 283 mg,
carbohydrates 7 g,
potassium 885 mg

TIME

10 minutes preparation
25 minutes cooking

INGREDIENTS

¼ cup unsalted butter, at room
temperature
2 shallots, finely chopped
Handful of fresh chives, finely snipped
Handful of fresh parsley sprigs, finely
chopped
Salt and freshly ground black pepper
to taste
6 salmon steaks, each ½ pound
½ cup dry white bread crumbs

Set the oven at 400 degrees. Use 1 tablespoon of the butter to grease a large shallow baking dish. Combine the remaining butter in a small bowl with the shallots, chives, parsley, and plenty of salt and pepper to taste.

Set the salmon in the baking dish ① and spread some of the herb mixture on each one ②. Sprinkle them with the bread crumbs ③ and bake in the preheated oven for 25 minutes or until the salmon is cooked through and the bread crumbs are golden. If necessary, slide the dish under the broiler for 1 minute to brown the bread crumbs. Serve at once with sautéed potatoes.

Fish Steaks with Soybeans and Snow Peas

YIELD

4 servings

Per serving
calories 556, protein 54 g,
fat 28 g, sodium 1091 mg,
carbohydrates 23 g, potassium
1744 mg

TIME

15 minutes preparation
30 minutes cooking

INGREDIENTS

1 cup dried soybeans
5 tablespoons peanut oil
4 halibut or salmon steaks, about
   1½–2 pounds
2 scallions (green and white parts),
   thinly sliced
1 teaspoon minced fresh gingerroot
3 tablespoons white wine or rice
   vinegar
3 tablespoons tamari or soy sauce
1 tablespoon sugar (optional)
¼ pound snow peas

Soak soybeans in water to cover overnight. Drain.

Heat oil in a large skillet and sauté fish steaks until lightly browned on both sides ①. Add scallions, ginger, wine, tamari, sugar (if desired), and soybeans. Cover tightly and simmer slowly for 20 minutes.

String snow peas ②. Add to simmering fish and cook 4 to 5 more minutes. The fish should flake easily when tested with a fork ③ and the soybeans should be crisp, the snow peas bright and firm.

Barbecued Fish Kabobs

YIELD

6 servings

Per serving
calories 410, protein 33 g,
fat 20 g, sodium 1044 mg,
carbohydrates 26 g,
potassium 1613 mg

TIME

15 minutes preparation
1 hour marinating
10 minutes grilling

INGREDIENTS

2 pounds thick firm fish, cubed
18 cherry tomatoes
18 small red potatoes, cooked
3 small zucchini, each cut into 6
   chunks
18 large mushrooms
1 large onion, cut in half and
   separated
3 large green peppers, cut into 1-inch
   squares

MARINADE

½ cup vegetable oil
¼ cup soy sauce
1 teaspoon chopped fresh ginger
1 clove garlic, minced
Black pepper
2 tablespoons dry sherry

Divide fish, tomatoes, potatoes, zucchini, mushrooms, onion, and green peppers into 6 equal portions. Thread 6 skewers alternating ingredients ① ②. Place skewers in a large, flat glass dish.

Combine marinade ingredients and baste skewers ③. Marinate 1 hour, turning occasionally.

Barbecue over hot coals for 10 minutes or until fish is done. Turn skewers once and brush occasionally with marinade.

NOTE These kabobs can also be broiled for the same amount of time. For the fish, use tuna, monkfish, pike, or sea trout.

New England Fish Pie

YIELD

4 servings

Per serving
calories 882, protein 31 g,
fat 61 g, sodium 937 mg,
carbohydrates 53 g,
potassium 712 mg

TIME

20 minutes preparation
45 minutes cooking

INGREDIENTS

1 pound fillets
1 cup water
¼ teaspoon salt
1 bay leaf
4 tablespoons butter or margarine
2 tablespoons minced celery
2 tablespoons minced onion
4 tablespoons all-purpose flour
2 cups half-and-half
¼ teaspoon dry mustard
¼ cup chopped walnuts

1 tablespoon dry white wine
1 tablespoon pimiento
Pastry for 2-crust 9-inch pie

In a large skillet place fish fillets, water, salt, and bay leaf. Bring water to a boil, reduce heat, cover, and simmer for 6 to 8 minutes.

Carefully remove fish, drain, cool, and flake. Discard poaching liquid.

Heat butter and sauté celery and onion; stir in flour and cook over low heat for 30 seconds.

Add half-and-half and dry mustard and cook, stirring constantly, until mixture thickens. Remove from heat and stir in nuts, wine, pimiento, and flaked fish.

Preheat oven to 400 degrees. Spoon mixture into pastry-lined 9-inch pie pan ①. Cover with top crust ②, trim, seal edges, and flute. Trim with extra pastry, if desired. Cut steam vents in top crust ③. Bake in hot oven for 30 to 35 minutes or until top is browned. Allow pie to stand for 15 minutes before cutting.

NOTE For this recipe, use fillets of cod, pollack, haddock, or ocean perch.

POULTRY

Roast Chicken with Lemon-Dill Sauce

YIELD

4 servings

Per serving
calories 475, protein 48 g,
fat 25 g, sodium 438 mg,
carbohydrates 6 g,
potassium 554 mg

TIME

10 minutes preparation
1½ hours cooking

INGREDIENTS

1 roasting chicken, about 3½ pounds
5 sprigs fresh dill or 1½ teaspoons dill
    weed
1 red onion, quartered
1 lemon, quartered
2 teaspoons butter
½ cup dry white wine
1 cup chicken broth
1 teaspoon cornstarch
Additional dill sprigs and lemon
    wedges to garnish

Preheat oven to 350 degrees.

Place chicken on roasting rack and put 4 sprigs (or 1 teaspoon dill weed) and quartered onion inside bird ①. Rub surface of chicken with lemon and spread with butter ②. Place 2 wedges of lemon inside, then place chicken in roasting pan and add wine and broth to pan. Roast for 1½ hours or until tender, basting with liquid every 15 to 20 minutes.

Transfer chicken from pan to a warmed platter and keep warm. Chop the remaining sprig of dill.

Strain the pan juices into a saucepan ③. Reserve 2 tablespoons of liquid and mix with the cornstarch until smooth. Pour cornstarch mixture into juices and bring to a boil. Whisk until smooth, add remaining dill and lemon, and then check for seasoning. Carve chicken and serve with sauce. Garnish with extra dill and lemon if desired.

Stuffed Roast Chicken

YIELD

4 to 6 servings

Per serving (4)
calories 794, protein 63 g,
fat 48 g, sodium 399 mg,
carbohydrates 25 g,
potassium 711 mg

TIME

20 minutes preparation
1 ½ hours cooking

INGREDIENTS

1 roasting chicken, about 4 pounds
1 tablespoon lemon juice
Salt and pepper to taste
2 tablespoons butter
1 small onion, minced
1 small clove garlic, minced
1 ½ cups cooked white rice
2 tablespoons chopped fresh parsley
2 tablespoons currants
¼ cup pine nuts (pignoli)

⅓ cup chopped walnuts
1 egg, lightly beaten
1 tablespoon tomato paste
¼ cup chicken broth, canned or fresh
1 tablespoon olive oil

Rinse chicken, inside and out, with cold water ①. Pat dry. Sprinkle inside with lemon juice and salt and pepper. Chop the raw liver. Pre-heat oven to 350 degrees.

In a skillet, heat butter and sauté the chopped chicken liver with the onion and garlic until light golden, about 2 minutes. Remove from heat and blend with all other ingredients except olive oil. Stuff chicken with the mixture ②, close the opening, and truss ③.

Rub chicken with olive oil, place in a roasting pan, and add about ⅓ cup water to the pan. Place in hot oven and roast for about 1 ½ hours, until tender and nicely browned. Baste with pan juices during cooking and add more water if needed. Allow to rest a few minutes before carving.

Grilled Chicken Tandoori

YIELD

4 servings

Per serving
calories 461, protein 49 g,
fat 25 g, sodium 238 mg,
carbohydrates 7 g,
potassium 554 mg

TIME

15 minutes preparation
Overnight marinating
20 minutes cooking

INGREDIENTS

1 chicken, about 3½ pounds, cut up
1 cup plain yogurt
2–3 cloves garlic, minced or
   crushed
½ teaspoon each ground cumin and
   ground cinnamon
1 teaspoon each ground turmeric,
   ginger, and coriander
¼ cup minced red onion
¼ cup fresh lime juice
Salt and freshly ground pepper
4 lime slices

Prick skin of chicken with a fork ①. Combine remaining ingredients, except lime slices, in a large, shallow bowl and add the chicken. Coat chicken pieces with the mixture ②; cover and refrigerate overnight. Turn once during the marinating ③.

Preheat broiler or prepare coals for grilling. Place chicken on barbecue or broiling rack set 3 to 4 inches from the heat. Cook until crisp and cooked on each side, about 8 minutes per side. Serve with lime slices.

NOTE Chicken may be baked in a 375-degree oven. Place chicken on lightly greased baking dish, skin side up, and bake for about 45 minutes, or until tender.

Lemon Chicken

YIELD

4 servings

Per serving
calories 556, protein 40 g,
fat 42 g, sodium 279 mg,
carbohydrates 3 g,
potassium 389 mg

TIME

20 minutes preparation
4 hours marinating
1 hour cooking

INGREDIENTS

1 chicken, about 3 pounds, cut in
   serving pieces
4 tablespoons olive oil
2 tablespoons grated onion
1 large clove garlic, crushed
1/2 teaspoon dried leaf thyme
1/2 teaspoon dried marjoram
1/2 teaspoon ground coriander
Peel of 1 lemon, grated
Juice of 1 lemon

1 teaspoon paprika
Salt and pepper to taste
3 tablespoon butter
2 tablespoons minced fresh parsley

In a bowl, blend all ingredients except butter and parsley. Rub the mixture well into the chicken pieces ① and let marinate for 4 hours. Turn the pieces in the marinade a few times ②.

Preheat the oven to 350 degrees.

Butter a baking dish, place chicken in 1 layer in the dish, and dot with pats of butter ③. Bake in hot oven for about 1 hour or until chicken is tender. Baste a few times with remaining marinade. Sprinkle chicken with parsley when serving.

Ragout of Chicken Legs

YIELD

Serves 4

Per serving
calories 708, protein 59 g,
fat 42 g, sodium 458 mg,
carbohydrates 6 g,
potassium 603 mg

TIME

15 minutes preparation
20 minutes cooking

INGREDIENTS

4 even-sized chicken legs
  (with thighs)
1 tablespoon oil
3 tablespoons butter
2 tablespoons flour
1/2 cup chicken stock
1 cup dry red wine
1 clove garlic, crushed
1 shallot, finely chopped
1 bay leaf

Salt and freshly ground black pepper
  to taste
2 tablespoons madeira wine
Bunch of watercress for garnish

Let the chicken legs sit at room temperature for 20 minutes. Heat the oil in a large skillet and add the butter. When the butter melts, brown the chicken legs a few at a time over a medium-high heat until they are all browned. Remove them from the pan and sprinkle in the flour ①. Cook, stirring, for 4 minutes, then pour in the chicken stock, wine, garlic, shallot, bay leaf, salt, pepper, and madeira ②. Bring the liquids to a boil, then replace the chicken legs skin side down ③ and cover the pan. Let the liquids return to the boil, then lower the heat and let the chicken simmer gently for 15 minutes or until the legs are cooked through.

Transfer the chicken legs to a platter and cover with foil; keep warm. Let the sauce return to a rolling boil and let it bubble vigorously until it is reduced by half. Remove the bay leaf and spoon the sauce over the chicken legs. Garnish with the watercress and serve at once.

NOTE The protruding knobs at the knuckle and thigh ends of the legs can be cut off with half-hole poultry shears.

Spicy Chicken and Walnut Stir-Fry

YIELD

4 servings

Per serving
calories 522, protein 40 g,
fat 28 g, sodium 2218 mg,
carbohydrates 24 g,
potassium 1185 mg

TIME

15 minutes preparation
30 minutes marinating
15 minutes cooking

INGREDIENTS

4 chicken legs (thigh and drumstick), boned
½ cup oyster sauce
2–3 cloves garlic, crushed
1 tablespoon grated gingerroot
1 each green and red bell pepper
1 small zucchini
1 yellow crookneck squash
1 tablespoon sesame or safflower oil
1 red or yellow onion, sliced
8 flowerets each broccoli and cauliflower
¼ cup sherry or chicken or beef broth
1–2 teaspoons sambel oelek (Indonesian chile paste)
½ cup walnut halves
2 tablespoons tamari or regular soy sauce
Cooked brown or white rice

Marinate the chicken legs for 30 minutes in a mixture of oyster sauce, garlic, and ginger ①.

Slice peppers and squashes into julienne strips and set aside.

Over medium-high heat, heat the sesame oil in a wok or large pan until almost smoking. Add the chicken and onion slices and toss ②, cooking for 3 to 4 minutes. Add the remaining ingredients ③. Stir to mix well and cook until vegetables are tender-crisp. Serve over brown or white rice.

Mancha Manteles

YIELD

6 servings

Per serving (without tortilla)

calories 717, protein 51 g, fat 40 g, sodium 1414 mg, carbohydrates 40 g, potassium 1199 mg

TIME

20 minutes preparation
1 to 1½ hours cooking

INGREDIENTS

⅔ cup all-purpose flour
2 teaspoons salt
½ teaspoon freshly ground pepper
1 3-pound chicken, cut up
1–2 tablespoons pork fat, lard, or vegetable oil
1 pound lean pork loin, cubed
¾ cup chopped walnuts
2 teaspoons sesame seeds
1 onion, diced
1 green pepper, seeded and diced
2 large tomatoes, peeled and cubed

½ teaspoon ground cumin
2 whole cloves
2 dried red chilies or 1 tablespoon mild chili (see note)
1 quart chicken stock
2 tart apples, peeled, cored, cubed
1 fresh pineapple
1 firm pear, peeled, cored, cubed
1 banana
½ ripe avocado
2 teaspoons lemon juice
Corn tortillas

Combine flour, salt, and pepper in a brown paper bag, then add chicken a piece at a time and shake to coat each piece ①. Set aside. Melt fat from the meat or use lard or oil to brown the pork cubes. Remove pork to a large kettle and add chicken pieces to fat. Brown well and transfer to kettle. Add nuts and sesame seeds to fat and sauté lightly ②, then add onion and green pepper. Cook, stirring occasionally, until soft and transparent; do not brown. Add tomatoes and cook a few minutes more to blend all ingredients.

Put cooked mixture in pan into blender jar and add cumin, cloves, chilies (or powder), and 2 tablespoons of stock. Blend until smooth purée and transfer to kettle with meat and chicken. Add remaining stock and simmer covered for 40 minutes.

Meanwhile peel and core the pineapple. Cut a quarter of it into ¼-inch wedges. Reserve remaining pineapple for another use. Add apples, pineapple wedges, and pear to kettle and simmer another 20 minutes. Peel and slice banana, then peel, seed, and slice avocado. Brush with lemon juice to prevent discoloring, then place on top of hot chicken and pork. Serve stew with corn tortillas (those sold in plastic packages are better than the canned).

NOTE Mild chili is made from pure ground red chilies with no additives and is available at many gourmet food shops. Regular chili powder can be substituted but taste is somewhat different.

Italian Drumsticks

YIELD

2 servings

Per serving
calories 479, protein 48 g,
fat 21 g, sodium 440 mg,
carbohydrates 20 g,
potassium 447 mg

TIME

10 minutes preparation
45 minutes cooking

INGREDIENTS

6 chicken drumsticks
Approximately 1 cup dry bread
   crumbs
1/4 cup grated parmesan cheese
Pinch of black pepper
Pinch of paprika
1 teaspoon Italian herbs
1/4 cup milk

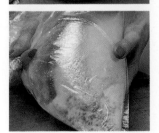
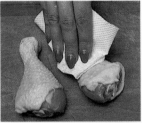

Preheat oven to 350 degrees. Line a baking sheet with aluminum foil.

Wash and pat chicken dry ①.

Mix bread crumbs, cheese, pepper, paprika, and Italian herbs in a double plastic bag.

Dip chicken in milk ②, then place in bag with crumbs and shake ③. Place chicken on baking sheet and bake in oven for approximately 45 minutes, or until browned and juices run clear when stuck with a fork.

Wrap 3 drumsticks for each person. Serve with a buttered Italian roll and a red pepper cut into quarters.

Braised Chicken Wings

YIELD

4 servings

Per serving
calories 367, protein 25 g,
fat 24 g, sodium 2065 mg,
carbohydrates 11 g,
potassium 291 mg

TIME

15 minutes preparation
30 minutes cooking

INGREDIENTS

2 pounds chicken wings
3 tablespoons cooking oil
6 tablespoons soy sauce
2 tablespoons dry sherry
1½ tablespoons honey
2 scallions (green and white parts),
    sliced
1 clove garlic, minced
¼ teaspoon freshly ground pepper

Cut wings through joints ①. Discard the wing tips or use for making chicken broth. In a skillet or wok, heat oil, and fry the chicken over high heat until nicely browned on both sides, about 3 or 4 minutes ②.

Combine all other ingredients. Pour off all but about 1 tablespoon fat from skillet, then add the mixture of ingredients, and coat the wing pieces with the mixture. Cover the skillet, reduce heat, and cook for about 25 minutes, or until the chicken is tender. Turn the pieces once during cooking and stir a few times to prevent the sauce from burning ③. When done, the chicken should be nicely glazed and practically no liquid left in the skillet.

Poached Chicken with Red Pepper Sauce

YIELD

Serves 6

Per serving
calories 426, protein 33 g,
fat 28 g, sodium 192 mg,
carbohydrates 3 g,
potassium 357 mg

TIME

30 minutes preparation
10 minutes cooking

INGREDIENTS

3 large whole boneless chicken breasts
1½ tablespoons butter
¾ cup white wine
1 cup heavy cream
1 tablespoon olive oil
1 red bell pepper, cut in thin strips
Salt and freshly ground black pepper
   to taste

Halve each chicken breast ① and trim away any fat ②. Use the butter to grease a large skillet and a piece of parchment paper or foil cut to fit the skillet exactly. Put the chicken in the pan, pour around the wine, and press the buttered paper or foil onto it ③. Cover with the lid and bring to a boil. Lower the heat so the liquid barely bubbles, and cook 8 minutes or until the chicken is opaque and firm to the touch. Transfer to a plate, reserving the cooking liquid; cover and keep warm.

Boil the cooking liquid until it is reduced to a thin film in the skillet. Pour in the cream, return to a boil, and let it bubble gently for 5 minutes. Set aside.

Heat the olive oil in another skillet and cook the pepper for a few minutes over a high heat. Pour in the cream mixture and stir thoroughly. Add salt and pepper to taste.

Arrange the chicken breasts on a platter like the spokes of a wheel. Spoon some sauce over each one and serve at once with rice pilaf.

Chicken in Parchment Paper

YIELD

Serves 4

Per serving
calories 554, protein 59 g,
fat 32 g, sodium 411 mg,
carbohydrates 4 g,
potassium 645 mg

TIME

15 minutes preparation
25 minutes cooking

INGREDIENTS

1 carrot, cut into matchsticks
6 tablespoons butter
1 leek, trimmed, washed thoroughly,
   and thinly sliced
1 stalk celery, cut into matchsticks
Salt and freshly ground black pepper
   to taste
4 whole boneless chicken breasts

Set the oven at 400 degrees. Put the carrots into a saucepan with cold water to cover and bring to a boil. Cook steadily for 2 minutes, then drain and rinse with cold water.

Cut 4 12-inch circles from cooking parchment and use 2 tablespoons of the butter to grease the circles to within 2 inches of the edges ①.

Melt the remaining butter in a skillet and cook the carrots, leeks, and celery with plenty of salt and pepper to taste over a medium heat for 3 minutes. Set aside for a few minutes to cool.

Remove the skin from the chicken breasts ② and discard any fat pockets on the meat. Divide the breasts in half and set both halves to one side of each piece of buttered parchment. Scatter some of the vegetables on each one and fold over the other half. Crimp the edges shut by turning the outside edge over and over onto itself ③. Set the packets on a baking sheet and bake in the preheated oven for 25 minutes or until the paper is puffed and the chicken feels firm to the touch through the paper.

Transfer quickly to plates and serve at once with buttered whole potatoes.

Chicken Tonnato

YIELD

6 servings

Per serving
calories 522, protein 50 g,
fat 36 g, sodium 596 mg,
carbohydrates 3 g,
potassium 508 mg

TIME

20 minutes preparation
25 minutes cooking
2–3 hours chilling

INGREDIENTS

6 chicken cutlets, about 2 pounds
Salt and pepper
Flour for dusting
$1/3$ cup butter or margarine
I can (6$1/2$ ounces) tuna, drained
2 cloves garlic
2 tablespoons anchovy paste
$1/2$ cup olive oil
$1/4$ cup red wine vinegar
$1/4$ cup heavy cream
Chopped parsley
Drained capers

Sprinkle chicken cutlets with salt and pepper. Dip chicken into flour and coat ①. Shake off all excess flour.

Heat butter in a large skillet and brown chicken breasts slowly until they are cooked, about 25 minutes. Remove from pan, drain on absorbent paper ②, and place on a serving platter. Cover and chill.

Place remaining ingredients except parsley and capers into a blender ③ and whirl until smooth. Pour sauce evenly over chicken and chill several hours.

Serve chicken sprinkled with parsley and capers, and accompanied by marinated tomato slices, artichoke hearts, and black olives.

Chicken Villeroi

YIELD

4 servings

Per serving
calories 428, protein 58 g,
fat 10 g, sodium 567 mg,
carbohydrates 17 g,
potassium 1057 mg

TIME

10 minutes preparation
15 minutes cooking

INGREDIENTS

1½ pounds chicken cutlets
Salt and freshly ground pepper
1 teaspoon each butter and oil
3 tablespoons finely chopped shallots
  or scallions
½ pound fresh mushrooms, quartered
  or sliced
2 tablespoons cognac or brandy
1 can (13 ounces) evaporated skim
  milk

½ cup shredded swiss cheese
½ cup crumbled low-fat farmers
  cheese
¼ cup grated parmesan cheese
Minced scallions

Cut each chicken cutlet into 6 or 7 strips ①. Sprinkle with salt and pepper.

Heat the butter and oil in a heavy skillet and when it is foaming, add the chicken strips. Cook over high heat, stirring and shaking the skillet for 3 to 4 minutes ②. Remove the chicken with a slotted spoon and set aside.

Add the shallots or scallions, mushrooms, and cognac and cook, stirring, for 2 or 3 minutes. Add the evaporated milk and cook down over high heat for about 5 minutes. Stir in the cheeses ③. Add chicken and heat through. Sprinkle parmesan cheese over entire dish and run under the broiler until golden brown. Garnish with scallions and serve hot.

Stir-Fried Chicken with Asparagus

YIELD

4 to 6 servings

Per serving (4)
calories 443, protein 20 g,
fat 35 g, sodium 804 mg,
carbohydrates 13 g,
potassium 532 mg

TIME

10 to 15 minutes
    preparation
30 minutes chilling
10 to 12 minutes cooking

INGREDIENTS

4–5 chicken thighs
1 teaspoon salt
1 tablespoon dry sherry
1 egg white
Cornstarch to coat
1 tablespoon oil
1 pound thin-stalked asparagus
3 cloves garlic
¾ cup chicken broth
1 tablespoon dry sherry
1 tablespoon cornstarch

3 tablespoons cold water
6–8 tablespoons oil for stir-frying
4–5 chunks gingerroot, about 1 inch
    thick
1 teaspoon oriental sesame oil

Remove the chicken meat from the bones ①. Trim the fat. Cut meat into uniform bite-sized pieces and place in a bowl. Add ½ teaspoon salt and the sherry. Mix well, then add the egg white. Mix again. Dust with cornstarch, and mix again. Refrigerate for at least 30 minutes. Bring to room temperature before cooking. If stuck together, coat with the 1 tablespoon oil to separate.

Snap off the tough ends of the asparagus. Cut the stalk on the bias into 1½-inch pieces, giving a quarter turn after each cut ②. Smash the ginger, peel the garlic and cut into thin slices. Combine the broth and sherry. Just before cooking, combine the cornstarch and water.

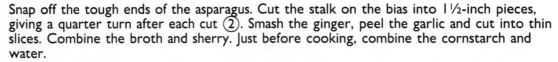

Heat a wok. Add 3 to 4 tablespoons oil. Heat for 30 seconds, then stir-fry the chicken ③ in 3 batches for 1½ to 2 minutes each, reheating the wok after each batch and adding more oil as necessary. Remove the chicken to a work platter with a strainer.

Add 1 to 2 tablespoons oil to the wok. Over high heat, lightly brown the ginger. Reduce the heat and add the garlic slices. Stir for 30 seconds, then add the remaining salt. Stir to mix well. Add the asparagus, then turn up the heat and stir for 1 minute. With a strainer, remove the contents of the wok to the platter.

Add the broth mixture to the wok and bring to the boil. Gradually add the cornstarch mixture, stirring constantly. When the consistency of honey is attained, add the chicken and asparagus. Stir to coat with sauce, then add the sesame oil. Mix and remove to a serving platter. Serve immediately.

VARIATION Cut 3 or 4 scallions to the size of the asparagus. Add after the ginger, and proceed with the recipe. Add a red bell pepper cut into 1-inch squares along with the asparagus.

Orange-Flavored Chicken, Sichuan Style

YIELD

4 to 6 servings

Per serving (4)
calories 490, protein 35 g,
fat 27 g, sodium 1298 mg,
carbohydrates 30 g,
potassium 717 mg

TIME

30 minutes preparation
30 minutes chilling
9 to 10 minutes cooking

INGREDIENTS

2 boned chicken breasts, 1 to 1¼
   pounds
1 teaspoon thin soy sauce
1 teaspoon dry sherry
1 egg white
Cornstarch to coat
Peel of 1 medium thin-skinned orange
3 scallions
6 tablespoons oil

1 bunch broccoli (flowerets only)
6 dried chili peppers
6 slices gingerroot, about ¼ inch thick

SAUCE

3 tablespoons dry sherry
3 tablespoons thin soy sauce
3 tablespoons red wine vinegar
1½ tablespoons sugar
1½ tablespoons orange juice

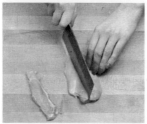

Trim the fat and gristle from the breasts and separate from the inner fillet ①. Cut the breasts lengthwise into 3 sections ②. Cut all sections on the bias into 1½-inch pieces ③. Place in a bowl and add the soy sauce and wine. Mix well. Add the egg white; mix again. Dust with cornstarch. Mix well and refrigerate at least 30 minutes. Bring to room temperature and coat with oil before cooking.

Hand-tear the orange peel into ½-inch pieces. Cut the scallions into ½-inch pieces. Place on a plate with the peppers, ginger, and orange peel. Blanch the broccoli flowerets, drain well, and reserve. Combine the sauce ingredients. Mix well.

Heat a wok and add ¼ cup oil. Heat for 1 minute or until white smoke appears, then stir-fry the chicken pieces in 3 batches for 45 seconds each batch. Allow the oil to reheat between batches and remove the chicken to your work platter with a strainer.

Add the remaining 2 tablespoons oil. Heat for 30 seconds, then add the peppers. Stir until lightly charred. Add the ginger slices, and stir 1 minute. Remove and discard both. Add the orange peel, stir for 1 minute, then add the scallions and stir for 30 seconds.

Mix the sauce and pour around the sides of the wok. Bring to the boil, add the chicken, then add the broccoli. Stir to mix well. Remove to a platter and serve immediately.

VARIATION *Thicken the sauce slightly by adding a mixture of 2 teaspoons cornstarch and 3 tablespoons sauce mixture; add to wok slowly, stirring constantly, when the sauce comes to the boil.*

Lu's Brunswick
Parslied B

YIELD

6 servings

Per serving
calories 564, protein 37 g,
fat 18 g, sodium 563 mg,
carbohydrates 67 g, potassium
1038 mg

TIME

15 minutes preparation
2¾ to 3 hours cooking

INGREDIENTS

1 3-pound broiler chicken, cut up
1 package each (10 ounces each)
    frozen corn, mixed vegetables, cut
    okra, and lima beans
1 can (16 ounces) whole tomatoes,
    with juice
½ teaspoon Tabasco
Salt and freshly ground black pepper

BIS

2 cu
1 tal
1 tea
⅔ c
⅓ c
2 tal

Place cut-up chicken in a 6- to 8-quart kettle. Cover with water and bring to a boil. Skim top if necessary. Reduce heat, cover, and simmer about 45 minutes to an 1 hour, or until chicken is tender.

Remove chicken from broth. Set aside until cool enough to handle. Skim fat from broth.

When chicken is cool, remove skin and bones and discard ①. Cut chicken into bite-size pieces ②, then return to the broth. Add all the vegetables, Tabasco, salt, and several grindings of black pepper. (This stew should have a peppery taste.) Simmer an hour or more; the longer this stew simmers, the more flavor it gains. Adjust seasonings, adding a little more black pepper, if necessary.

As stew simmers, prepare the biscuits. Preheat oven to 425 degrees. Combine dry ingredients in a sifter and sift into a large bowl. Add the milk and oil and parsley on top of flour. Mix thoroughly until the mixture pulls away from the sides of the bowl and forms a ball ③. Drop dough from the end of a spoon onto ungreased baking sheet, and bake for 10 to 12 minutes or until golden brown.

Chicken and Oysters on Cornbread

YIELD

6 servings

Per serving (with 1 square cornbread)

calories 498, protein 31 g, fat 22 g, sodium 906 mg, carbohydrates 40 g, potassium 458 mg

TIME

30 minutes preparation
20 minutes cooking

INGREDIENTS

4 tablespoons butter
5 tablespoons all-purpose flour
1¾ cups chicken stock
½ cup light cream
½ teaspoon salt
4 or 5 drops Tabasco
1½ pints shucked oysters
2 cups chopped cooked chicken
2 tablespoons minced fresh parsley

CORNBREAD

¾ cup yellow cornmeal
1 cup all-purpose flour
¼ cup sugar
3 teaspoons baking powder
¼ teaspoon salt
1 cup milk
1 egg, well beaten
2 tablespoons butter or margarine, melted

Preheat oven to 425 degrees.

Prepare cornbread. In large bowl, combine and mix cornmeal, flour, sugar, baking powder, and salt.

Add milk, egg, and butter; blend well ①. Pour into a greased, 8-inch square baking pan and bake 20 minutes.

While cornbread bakes, make a white sauce by melting the butter, adding the flour, and stirring until smooth ②. Remove from heat, add stock and blend. Simmer over low heat about 5 minutes. Add cream, salt, and Tabasco.

Poach the oysters in their liquid until the edges curl and they are plump ③, about 5 minutes or less. Drain and add to sauce with chicken. Serve on squares of freshly made cornbread, split like short-cake, with sauce in the middle and on top. Sprinkle with parsley.

Mole Mexicano

YIELD

6 servings

Per serving
calories 446, protein 41 g,
fat 23 g, sodium 1197 mg,
carbohydrates 18 g,
potassium 802 mg

TIME

30 minutes preparation
1½ hours cooking

INGREDIENTS

1 roasting chicken about 4 pounds,
    cut up
Celery tops
1 carrot, quartered
1 medium Spanish onion, half
    quartered and half chopped
2 teaspoons salt
1 slice dry bread
2 tablespoons seedless raisins
½ ounce (½ square) unsweetened
    chocolate
¼ cup blanched almonds
1 cup finely chopped green pepper
2 cups quartered fresh tomato
1 garlic clove, minced
3 tablespoons flour
¼ teaspoon ground cinnamon
1 tablespoon ground pure hot red
    chile
¼ teaspoon ground cloves
2½ cups chicken broth

Place chicken in a pot, add cold water to barely cover. Add celery tops, carrot, quartered half onion, and salt. Cover and cook until tender, about 1 hour. Set aside and cool.

Using a food processor, electric blender, or mortar and pestle, grind chopped onion, bread, raisins, chocolate, almonds, green pepper, tomato, and garlic ①. Stir in flour and spices, then add chicken broth and mix until well blended ②.

Cook sauce until slightly thickened. Taste and adjust seasonings. Add chicken pieces ③ and simmer gently for 30 minutes, basting frequently. Serve with steamed rice. Leftovers are wonderful for filling tacos, omelettes, or tamales.

Country Chicken Pie

YIELD

6 servings

Per serving
calories 687, protein 39 g,
fat 43 g, sodium 1648 mg,
carbohydrates 36 g,
potassium 696 mg

TIME

30 minutes preparation
2 hours cooking

INGREDIENTS

1 roasting chicken or fowl, about 4 to
  5 pounds
1 clove garlic
½ teaspoon black peppercorns
1 large onion studded with 5 cloves
1 stalk celery, coarsely chopped
1 tablespoon salt
3 carrots, scraped and cut in 1-inch
  pieces
12 small white onions, peeled
6 large fresh mushrooms
¾ cup butter
⅔ cup all-purpose flour
½ cup cooked peas
1 tablespoon chopped fresh parsley
Rich pie crust for 9-inch pan
1 egg, well beaten
1 tablespoon heavy cream

In a large kettle, bring chicken to a boil in water to cover. Add garlic, peppercorns, onion, celery, and salt. Lower heat, cover, and simmer about 1 hour or until chicken is tender. Remove chicken. Discard celery and large onion. Skim any fat, then bring broth to boil. Add carrots, white onions, and mushrooms. Remove mushrooms after 10 minutes and slice. Set aside. Cook broth 5 minutes more, then strain; measure 4 cups and set aside. Save remainder for another use. Set carrots and onions aside. Preheat oven to 400 degrees.

Melt butter in a heavy skillet over medium heat. Add flour and cook, stirring constantly. Gradually stir in broth until thickened and smooth, about 1 minute. Remove from heat and season to taste.

Remove chicken from bones in large pieces and place into a 1-quart casserole. Add sauce and vegetables along with peas and scatter parsley on top.

Roll pie crust until ¼ inch thick and wide enough to fit with a 1-inch overhang ①. Place on pie with edges under and crimp edges ②. Cut steam vents. Combine egg with cream and brush on crust ③. Bake in hot oven for 45 minutes or until golden.

Chicken Livers with Cauliflower and Red Pepper

YIELD

4 to 6 servings

Per serving (4)
calories 353, protein 27 g,
fat 20 g, sodium 1058 mg,
carbohydrates 18 g,
potassium 688 mg

TIME

20 to 25 minutes
    preparation
5 to 6 minutes cooking

INGREDIENTS

1 pound chicken livers
Cornstarch to coat
3 knobs gingerroot, 1 inch long
2 scallions
1 small head cauliflower
1 teaspoon salt
1 large red bell pepper
4–5 tablespoons oil

SAUCE

2 tablespoons oyster sauce
2 teaspoons A-1 Sauce
2 teaspoons dry sherry
Ground pepper

Trim the livers of fat and membranes ①. Discard mealy pieces. Place livers in a bowl, coat with cornstarch, and mix. Smash the ginger. Wash, trim, and cut scallions into 1-inch pieces.

Break the cauliflower heads into uniform bite-sized pieces ②. Bring 2 quarts water to the boil, add 1 teaspoon salt, and blanch the cauliflower for 45 seconds. Drain, cool, and dry.

Cut the red pepper into 1-inch squares. Combine the sauce ingredients.

Heat a wok. Add 3 tablespoons oil, heat for 30 seconds, then add ginger. Stir and cook until browned; discard. Add half the livers. Stir until browned and lightly spongy when pressed with the spatula. Remove to a work platter. Cook the remaining livers, adding oil down the sides ③ of wok if necessary. Remove.

Add the scallions and peppers; stir 30 seconds. Add the cauliflower and livers; stir 15 seconds. Pour the sauce down the sides of the wok, stirring to coat thoroughly. Remove to a platter and serve immediately.

Stewed Capon with Capers

YIELD

5 to 6 servings

Per serving
calories 838, protein 56 g,
fat 31 g, sodium 603 mg,
carbohydrates 67 g, potassium
781 mg

TIME

20 minutes preparation
2 hours cooking

INGREDIENTS

1 5-pound capon, turkey, or stewing
  chicken, cut up .
2 cups dry white wine
Salt
5 peppercorns
1 carrot, diced
1 stalk celery (no leaves), diced
1 Spanish onion, sliced
1 small turnip, sliced
2 sprigs fresh parsley

⅛ teaspoon crumbled dried rosemary
2 tablespoons butter
2 tablespoons flour
⅓ cup drained capers
2 pimientos, cut in strips
¼ cup sliced pitted green olives
1 egg yolk
Juice ½ lemon
1 pound broad noodles, cooked

Place capon in 4- to 6-quart kettle. Add wine and enough water to cover. Season with salt and peppercorns, cover, and simmer for 30 minutes. Skim broth with large kitchen spoon, then add carrot, celery, onion, turnip, parsley, and rosemary and continue to simmer covered until bird is tender, about 1 to 1½ hours.

Remove capon and keep warm. Strain broth through a sieve lined with 2 layers of cheesecloth, pressing down on back of spoon to remove all juices from vegetables ①. Return liquid to kettle. Cover to keep warm.

In a saucepan over a *low* flame, melt the butter and blend with flour, stirring slowly until! golden brown ②. Add this roux to sauce to thicken it, stirring all the time ③. Add capers, pimientos, and olives and stir.

Return capon to kettle. Mix egg yolk with lemon juice. Add to this mixture about 2 or 3 tablespoons of the warm thickened broth and mix well. Pour over the capon, and heat through. Serve with plain noodles.

Cornish Hens with Rosemary

YIELD

Serves 6

Per serving
calories 501, protein 53 g,
fat 29 g, sodium 236 mg,
carbohydrates 1 g,
potassium 462 mg

TIME

20 minutes preparation
40 minutes cooking

INGREDIENTS

6 Cornish hens, thawed if necessary
Salt and freshly ground black pepper
   to taste
About ½ cup sour cream
2 teaspoons dried rosemary

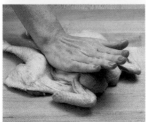

Set the oven at 425 degrees.

Take the giblets from the hens and reserve them for another use. Pull out the pockets of fat at the opening and set the birds breast side down on a board. Use poultry shears to cut up either side of the backbone on each bird, lifting out and discarding them ①. Separate the 2 cut sides so the hens are almost flat. Turn them over and press firmly with the heel of your hand right in the center of the breastbone so the hens lie completely flat ②. Tuck the wing pinions back to expose the breasts and bend up the "knees" of the hens so they are even on both sides ③.

Put the hens into a large roasting pan skin side up and sprinkle them with salt and pepper. Rub some of the sour cream onto each bird. Crush the rosemary in the palm of your hand and sprinkle some rosemary onto each one.

Bake the hens in the preheated oven for 40 minutes or until they are golden brown on top and cooked through. Transfer each to a dinner plate and serve with sautéed snow peas.

Spicy Roast Duck

YIELD

4 to 6 servings

Per serving (4)
calories 796, protein 43 g,
fat 61 g, sodium 1946 mg,
carbohydrates 14 g,
potassium 578 mg

TIME

25 minutes preparation
1 hour marinating
2½ hours cooking

INGREDIENTS

1 duckling, about 5 pounds
⅓ cup soy sauce
2 tablespoons dry sherry
2 tablespoons dark corn syrup
2 tablespoons grated onion
1 clove garlic, crushed
1 teaspoon grated gingerroot
½ teaspoon dry mustard
¼ teaspoon ground allspice
2 teaspoons cider vinegar

½ cup dry white wine
Salt and pepper to taste
2 teaspoons cornstarch mixed with 2
    tablespoons water

Remove any loose fat from duck cavity; rinse duck with cold water and dry with paper towel. Combine all other ingredients except cornstarch. Pour half the mixture into the duck cavity ①, coating the inner surface, then close the opening with skewers and string. Rub the remaining mixture into the duck skin ②, and let stand for 1 hour.

Preheat oven to 325 degrees.

Place duck on a rack in a roasting pan. Add 1 inch of water to the pan. Prick the duck skin in several places with a sharp fork. Roast in hot oven for 2 hours; add more water to pan if needed. Brush a few times with pan juices during roasting. After 2 hours, remove pan from oven, and remove trussing from duck. Let all juices from the cavity run into the pan. Pour pan juices into a bowl, remove rack, and place duck back into pan and roast for another 30 minutes.

Skim fat from the pan juices ③. A few minutes before the duck is done, place pan juices into a small saucepan, add the cornstarch mixture, and simmer while stirring until the sauce has thickened. Spoon sauce over the bird before serving.

Duck with Cranberries

YIELD

8 servings

Per serving
calories 884, protein 45 g,
fat 62 g, sodium 918 mg,
carbohydrates 34 g,
potassium 719 mg

TIME

30 minutes preparation
2 hours cooking

INGREDIENTS

2 ducklings, about 5 pounds each
1 small onion, peeled and quartered
1 stalk celery, scraped and sliced
1 medium carrot, scraped
1 teaspoon salt
½ teaspoon dried thyme
1 bay leaf
5 cups water or chicken broth
¼ cup cornstarch
⅔ cup sugar

½ cup dry white wine
1½ pounds fresh cranberries
Salt to taste
Watercress for garnish

Preheat the oven to 450 degrees.

Rinse ducks; remove excess fat from body and save; cut off wing tips ①. Place on rack in roasting pan, then prick skin near wings with a fork ②. Roast uncovered in hot oven 15 minutes. Spoon off any fat in pan, lower heat to 350 degrees, and cook 1¼ hours more.

Meanwhile, in a saucepan, render duck fat over medium heat until you have 2 tablespoons. Sauté giblets, necks, and wing tips in fat until golden ③. Add onion, celery, carrot, salt, herbs, and water. Bring to a boil, then reduce heat and simmer 1 hour. Pass duck stock through cheesecloth-lined strainer. Discard solids and set aside 1 cup stock.

Remove ducks from oven, turn upside down, and place on broiler rack; pour off any fat. Broil until crisp and brown, about 5 minutes, then remove to platter. Let rest 15 minutes.

In a stainless steel or enamel saucepan, combine cornstarch and sugar; stir in wine and cranberries. Cook until slightly thickened and berries are soft, about 10 minutes. Stir in reserved stock and add salt to taste. Serve over roasted duck. Garnish with watercress.

Barbecued Rotisserie Turkey

YIELD

8 servings

Per serving
calories 624, protein 76 g,
fat 24 g, sodium 471 mg,
carbohydrates 24 g,
potassium 827 mg

TIME

10 minutes preparation
3 hours grilling

INGREDIENTS

1 turkey, about 10 pounds, thawed if
    frozen
Salt and pepper
½ cup melted butter or margarine
2 cloves garlic, mashed
Juice of 1 lemon and 1 orange
1 cup jellied cranberry sauce, mashed
¼ cup prepared mustard
¼ cup honey

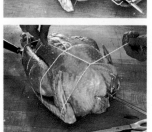

Build the fire arranging the coals at the back of the rotisserie and with a long, narrow drip pan at the front.

Sprinkle turkey inside and out with salt and pepper. Pass the rotisserie rod through the neck skin and then to a point just above the tail ①. Fasten ends. Tie wings and legs close to the body with string ②. If desired, place a meat thermometer into the thickest part of the thigh, not touching a bone ③.

Place turkey 8 inches above gray coals and let rotate for 2 to 2½ hours, adding more coals from time to time.

Combine remaining ingredients and brush over turkey every 5 minutes. Grill for another 30 to 40 minutes or until richly browned.

If any sauce remains, heat it in a pan on the grill and spoon over each serving. Serve with brown-and-serve biscuits baked on grill, foil-baked succotash, and baked sweet potatoes.

This turkey can also be made very successfully on a dome-type covered grill. See manufacturer's instructions for specifics.

NOTE If you are using a meat thermometer, allow turkey to cook until it registers 180°F.

BEEF AND VEAL

Texas Barbecued Beef

YIELD

6 servings

Per serving
calories 1624, protein 79 g,
fat 46 g, sodium 2386 mg,
carbohydrates 205 g,
potassium 1284 mg

TIME

30 minutes preparation
2 hours marinating
30 minutes grilling

INGREDIENTS

3 stalks celery, approximately
4 large onions, approximately
3 cups dry red wine, such as Chianti
1 can (10½ ounces) condensed beef
   broth
1 can (6 ounces) tomato paste
2 tablespoons Worcestershire sauce
2 cups chili sauce
1 boneless chuck steak, about 3
   pounds
12 hero rolls, split

Finely chop the celery so that you have 2 cups; chop the onions finely to have 2 cups ①.

Mix onions and celery with wine, beef broth concentrate, tomato paste, Worcestershire sauce, and chili sauce until well blended. Cook mixture in a saucepan for 20 to 25 minutes, then press mixture through a sieve ②. Cool.

Place chuck steak in a shallow pan or glass dish. Pour marinade over top. Turn steak in marinade several times ③ and allow to marinate for 2 hours at room temperature.

Drain the steak, reserving the marinade. Place steak on grill 6 inches above gray coals. Grill 30 minutes, brushing with marinade and turning every 5 minutes.

Heat the remaining marinade and keep warm. Toast rolls on grill.

Cut the beef into paper-thin slices and place on rolls. Spoon hot marinade over meat and replace tops of buns. Serve at once with potato salad, three-bean salad, and grilled whole frying peppers.

Fillet Steaks with Mock Bearnaise

YIELD

Serves 4

Per serving
calories 805, protein 44 g,
fat 68 g, sodium 318 mg,
carbohydrates 2 g,
potassium 823 mg

TIME

10 minutes preparation
10 minutes cooking

INGREDIENTS

4 fillet steaks, cut 1½ inches thick
2 tablespoons oil
Salt and freshly ground black pepper
   to taste
Small bunch of watercress for garnish

SAUCE

2 tablespoons lemon juice
3 egg yolks
Salt and freshly ground black pepper
   to taste
¾ cup unsalted butter, cut up
1 shallot, very finely chopped
1 teaspoon chopped fresh tarragon or
   chopped vinegar-preserved
   tarragon

Let the fillet steaks sit at room temperature for 20 minutes. Heat the oil in a large skillet and when it is quite hot, add the steaks with salt and pepper to taste and cook over a fairly high heat, turning them every minute until they have cooked for 6 minutes altogether (for rare steak), 8 minutes (for medium steak), and 10 minutes (for well-done steak).

Meanwhile, put the lemon juice and egg yolks in the container of a blender or food processor and add salt and pepper to taste ①. Melt the butter, turn on the machine, remove the insert cap, and drizzle in the hot butter in a slow steady stream ②. When it is all incorporated, turn off the machine, add the chopped shallots and tarragon ③, and turn the machine on for less than 5 seconds just to combine them.

Arrange a fillet steak on each plate and pour the mock Bearnaise on the side of each steak. Garnish with watercress and serve at once.

Salt-and-Pepper-Crusted Steak

YIELD

6 to 8 servings

Per serving (6)
calories 1084, protein 58 g,
fat 92 g, sodium 1385 mg,
carbohydrates 2 g,
potassium 683 mg

TIME

10 minutes preparation
30 minutes marinating
50 minutes grilling

INGREDIENTS

1 boneless sirloin steak, 3 inches
   thick, about 4 to 5 pounds
1/3 cup each corn oil and prepared
   mustard
Coarse salt, about 1 cup
2 tablespoons cracked black
   peppercorns

Trim excess fat from steak. Slash the fatty edge of the steak to keep it from curling ①.

Mix oil and mustard and spread it in a thick layer over the steak, top and bottom ②.

Mix salt with pepper and coat steak with mixture, pressing the layer firmly onto the steak ③. Place steak on wax paper and let stand for 30 minutes at room temperature.

Place steak 6 inches above gray coals and grill for 20 minutes on each side for rare, 25 minutes for medium. Use tongs to turn the steak to keep from piercing the meat.

Break the crust from the steak and cut meat into thin slices across the grain. Serve as is or on rye bread toast. Good with corn relish, baked potatoes with chive butter, and beefsteak tomatoes.

Saucy Korean Ribs

YIELD

2 to 3 servings

Per serving (3)
calories 530, protein 21 g,
fat 46 g, sodium 2949 mg,
carbohydrates 6 g, potassium
492 mg

TIME

10 minutes preparation
2 hours cooking

INGREDIENTS

2 pounds beef ribs, cut 3 inches long
6 tablespoons soy sauce
3 cloves garlic, minced
4–5 scallions (green and white parts),
    chopped
1 tablespoon sesame seeds
1/8 teaspoon salt

Score the beef ribs on both sides about one-third of the way down ①; Do not cut all the way through. Put ribs in a heavy kettle.

Add the garlic to the soy sauce and put in kettle along with enough water to cover the ribs three-fourths of the way up ②. Add the scallions.

Toast the sesame seeds in salt briefly until rounded and brown ③. Add to ribs. Bring to a boil, lower the heat to simmer, cover, and cook slowly for 2 hours or until done. Serve with boiled white rice.

London Broil with Ratatouille Salad

YIELD

6 servings

Per serving
calories 714, protein 49 g,
fat 49 g, sodium 909 mg,
carbohydrates 18 g,
potassium 1255 mg

TIME

15 minutes preparation
50 minutes cooking
1–2 hours chilling

INGREDIENTS

1 london broil, about 3 pounds
1 clove garlic, crushed
2 teaspoons cracked pepper
2 tablespoons olive oil
1 cup garlic-flavored vinaigrette
1 green pepper
1 large onion
2 garlic cloves
1 large eggplant
2 zucchini

½ pound mushrooms
1 can (1 pound) tomatoes with juice
Salt and pepper

Spread london broil with garlic, pepper, and oil ①. Broil for 10 minutes on each side for rare, 12 minutes for medium. Cool and then chill.

Chop the green pepper, slice the onion, and mince the garlic. Leave skin on eggplant, but cut away stem and chop into medium dice ②. Slice the zucchini and wipe the mushrooms clean with a damp towel and then slice.

Place vinaigrette dressing into a large saucepan. Add chopped vegetables and tomatoes with the juice. Simmer uncovered until vegetables are soft and mushy, about 30 minutes. Season to taste with salt and pepper. Cool and then chill.

When ready to serve, cut london broil into thin slices ③ and serve with ratatouille salad. Have crusty rolls and chive butter alongside.

London Broil Pinwheels

YIELD

4 servings

Per serving
calories 562, protein 59 g,
fat 20 g, sodium 6014 mg,
carbohydrates 20 g,
potassium 1206 mg

TIME

20 minutes preparation
2 hours marinating
10 minutes grilling

INGREDIENTS

1 flank steak, about 2 pounds
Seasoned instant meat tenderizer
1 clove garlic, mashed
4 scallions, minced
1 cup dry sherry
1 cup Japanese soy sauce
¼ cup tomato paste
8 slices monterey jack cheese
8 cling peach halves

Pound flank steak until it is ½ inch thick ①.

Sprinkle the meat with tenderizer, garlic, and scallions. Roll up meat lengthwise tightly like a jelly roll ②.

Cut meat roll into 8 slices and spear each slice on a skewer ③.

Place skewers into a shallow glass dish. Mix sherry, soy sauce, and tomato paste until smooth; pour over meat. Turn skewers and let marinate for 2 hours at room temperature.

Drain skewers and reserve marinade. Place skewers 4 inches above gray coals and grill for 5 minutes on each side, brushing with marinade every few minutes.

Dip the cheese slices into the marinade and place over meat. Grill until cheese melts.

Dip the peaches into the marinade and grill for 2 to 3 minutes on each side. Serve with hot pita bread and a green bean and red onion salad.

New England Boiled Dinner

YIELD

4 servings

Per serving
calories 1237, protein 68 g,
fat 82 g, sodium 2910 mg,
carbohydrates 56 g,
potassium 1896 mg

TIME

30 minutes preparation
3½ hours cooking

INGREDIENTS

1 corned beef brisket (3½ pounds)
2 medium onions, peeled
2 medium potatoes
4 large carrots, scraped
4 parsnips, peeled
1 large yellow turnip or rutabaga,
   peeled and sliced
6 small beets, scrubbed
1 medium green cabbage, cored and
   quartered
1 teaspoon salt

Cover beef with water in a 4- to 6-quart casserole and bring to simmer over medium heat. Cook 2 hours, skimming any foam ①. Add onions and potatoes and boil 15 minutes. Add carrots, parsnips, and turnips and boil 30 minutes more.

Meanwhile, boil beets in salted water for 30 minutes until tender; drain, peel ②, and keep warm.

Remove meat from casserole, slice ③, and arrange slices on a warm platter with vegetables around it. Place in a warm oven along with beets.

Turn up heat under broth and, when boiling, add cabbage and cook 3 to 7 minutes, to taste. Drain and place on platter with other vegetables or in a separate serving dish if desired. Serve with horseradish, mustard, and pickles. Or mix 1 part horseradish with 2 parts sour cream for a tangy horseradish sauce.

Carbonnade

YIELD

4 servings

Per serving
calories 620, protein 63 g,
fat 27 g, sodium 532 mg,
carbohydrates 17 g,
potassium 1201 mg

TIME

30 minutes preparation
2 hours cooking

INGREDIENTS

3 tablespoons oil
2½ pounds sirloin tip or chuck roast,
*   cut into ¾-inch slices*
2 large onions, thinly sliced
2 cloves garlic, minced
Salt and pepper
4 sprigs fresh parsley
1 bay leaf
½ teaspoon dried leaf thyme
½ teaspoon dried marjoram

Pinch of grated nutmeg
1 cup beef broth, canned or fresh
1 tablespoon tomato paste
2 tablespoons red wine vinegar
3 cups beer or ale (approximately)
2 tablespoons cornstarch
3 tablespoons water

In a heavy skillet, heat oil over high heat. Sauté the beef slices quickly to brown on both sides ①. Remove from pan and reserve.

Reduce heat and sauté onions slowly until golden and soft. Add garlic and sauté 1 minute longer.

Cover the bottom of an ovenproof casserole with half the meat slices ②; season with a little salt and pepper, then cover with half the sautéed onions, the remaining beef, and then the rest of the onions.

Preheat oven to 325 degrees.

Tie parsley, bay leaf, thyme leaves, marjoram, and nutmeg in a piece of cheesecloth ③. Add to casserole, then add beef broth and tomato paste, vinegar, and enough beer or ale to just cover the meat and onions. Bring to a simmer on top of the stove, then place in hot oven and cook for about 1½ hours or until meat is tender. Remove meat from casserole to a serving dish and keep warm. Remove and discard cheesecloth bag with herbs.

Place casserole over moderately high heat. Let the sauce come to a simmer. Dissolve cornstarch in water, and add to the simmering sauce. Stir well and simmer until the sauce has thickened. Pour sauce over meat and serve.

Polish Beef and Vegetable Stew

YIELD

4 servings

Per serving
calories 499, protein 39 g,
fat 29 g, sodium 457 mg,
carbohydrates 22 g,
potassium 964 mg

TIME

20 minutes preparation
1 hour, 30 minutes
   cooking

INGREDIENTS

1½-pound piece brisket of beef
¼ cup all-purpose flour
2 tablespoons butter
1 cup beef broth, canned or fresh
1 large onion, coarsely chopped
3 carrots, pared and sliced
1 parsnip, pared and sliced
⅓ cup chopped fresh parsley
2 stalks celery (white part only), sliced

Salt and pepper
¾ cup sour cream
1 tablespoon chopped fresh dill leaves
   or 2 teaspoons dillweed

Cut meat into ¾-inch-thick slices ①, then dredge lightly with flour ②. In a saucepan, heat butter. Brown meat quickly on both sides, then add broth, cover and cook gently for 1 hour. Add vegetables, season with salt and pepper, and add a little more broth if too dry. Cover and simmer for another 30 minutes.

Correct seasoning and remove from heat. Stir in sour cream ③, sprinkle with dill, and serve.

Fruited Meat and Fragrant Rice

YIELD

6 servings

Per serving
calories 1055, protein 38 g,
fat 45 g, sodium 251 mg,
carbohydrates 124 g, potassium
1222 mg

TIME

20 minutes preparation
Overnight marinating
1½ to 2 hours cooking

INGREDIENTS

2 pounds stew beef, in 1-inch cubes
2 cups dark beer
2 tablespoons butter
1 tablespoon peanut or vegetable oil
Salt and freshly ground black pepper
½ teaspoon crumbled dried thyme
1 bay leaf
¾ pound pitted dates, or 1 pound
   with pits to be removed
¼ pound currants or raisins
¼ pound dried apricots

FRAGRANT RICE

2 cups brown rice
5 cups water
Salt and freshly ground black pepper
½ teaspoon ground cinnamon
3 tablespoons butter
2 tablespoons finely chopped, firmly
   packed fresh mint leaves or parsley
   or mixed mint and parsley
   (not dried)
¼ pound unsalted roasted cashews,
   coarsely chopped

Place meat in a bowl. Add beer, cover bowl, and refrigerate overnight. Preheat oven to 325 degrees. Drain beef and reserve the marinade. Pat meat dry with paper towels ①.

Heat the butter and oil in a heavy ovenproof casserole. Brown meat a few pieces at a time, making sure that pieces do not touch ②. (This keeps the meat from losing juices.) Keep turning and browning on all sides. Sprinkle with salt and freshly ground pepper to taste. Remove from heat.

Sprinkle in thyme, then add bay leaf and fruits. Cover tightly. Bake 1 to 1½ hours. Look at the meat occasionally; if it appears dry, add a little of the reserved marinade to keep it moist ③.

While meat cooks, prepare the rice. Put all ingredients except nuts in a heavy saucepan and bring to a boil. Stir to combine, cover, and simmer until all the liquid is absorbed, about 45 minutes. Stir in nuts. Remove bay leaf from the meat and serve over the fragrant rice.

NOTE *If you soak the brown rice for 2 hours in cold water, reduce the cooking time to 30 minutes and cook in the soaking liquid.*

Beef with Broccoli in Black Bean Sauce

YIELD

4 to 6 servings

Per serving (4)
calories 501, protein 33 g,
fat 31 g, sodium 1216 mg,
carbohydrates 25 g,
potassium 996 mg

TIME

5 to 10 minutes
preparation
30 minutes chilling
8 to 10 minutes cooking

INGREDIENTS

1-pound strip flank steak
2 teaspoons thin soy sauce
2 teaspoons dry sherry
1 egg white
Cornstarch to coat
Oil for stir-frying
1 bunch broccoli
salt
2 tablespoons salted black beans
2 cloves garlic
1 teaspoon dry sherry

2 tablespoons cornstarch
1 cup sliced bamboo shoots

SAUCE

3/4 cup chicken broth
1 tablespoon black soy sauce
2 tablespoons oyster sauce
2 teaspoons dry sherry
2 teaspoons sugar

Chill the steak until firm but not frozen. Cut on the bias into very thin slices about 2 inches by 1 inch ①. Place in a bowl and add the soy sauce and sherry. Mix well, add the egg white, and mix again. Dust with cornstarch ②. Mix and refrigerate at least 30 minutes. Bring to room temperature before cooking, and coat with oil.

Separate the flowerets from the broccoli stalk. Break the flowerets into uniform pieces, then remove the tough outer skin from the stalk with a paring knife ③. Cut the stalk on the bias into 1/8-inch slices.

Place a colander in the sink. Bring 10 cups of water to the boil, add a pinch of salt, then add the broccoli. Remove broccoli to the colander when it turns dark green (no longer than 15 seconds). Rinse with cold water immediately to stop the cooking, and pat or spin dry. Reserve for later.

Rinse the black beans under hot water. Peel and mince the garlic. Combine with the beans and moisten with the sherry. Combine the sauce ingredients. Remove 5 tablespoons of sauce and combine with the cornstarch. Do this just before beginning to cook.

Heat a wok. Add 4 tablespoons oil. Swirl about for 30 seconds, then stir-fry the beef in 3 batches, for 30 to 45 seconds each batch and adding more oil as necessary, allowing it to re-heat before adding meat. Using a strainer, remove the beef to a platter. Add more oil if necessary, heat, then add the beans and garlic. Stir for 15 seconds, then add the broccoli and bamboo shoots. Stir for 30 seconds. Remove to the platter.

Add 1 tablespoon oil, heat, and add the sauce. Bring to the boil, gradually add the cornstarch mixture stirring constantly, and thicken to the consistency of honey. Add the beef and vegetables, stir to coat with sauce, and serve.

Pennsylvania Dutch Cabbage Rolls

YIELD

6 servings

Per serving
calories 410, protein 21 g,
fat 26 g, sodium 850 mg,
carbohydrates 23 g,
potassium 852 mg

TIME

40 minutes preparation
1 hour, 15 minutes
  cooking

INGREDIENTS

12 large green cabbage leaves
1¼ pound ground beef
1 cup cooked rice
1 small onion, chopped
1 teaspoon salt
1 egg
2 tablespoons vegetable oil
2 cans (8 ounces) tomato sauce
¼ cup water
1 tablespoon brown sugar
1 tablespoon lemon juice or vinegar

Pour boiling water over cabbage leaves and soak until limp, about 4 minutes.

Combine beef, rice, onion, salt, and egg and mix well. Divide mixture into 12 equal portions and place one portion on each leaf ①. Roll up ②, tuck ends in, and fasten with toothpicks ③.

Heat oil in a heavy skillet or Dutch oven and brown the cabbage rolls 10 minutes. Combine tomato sauce, water, brown sugar, and lemon juice and add to skillet. Simmer cabbage rolls 1 hour, covered, then serve hot.

Surprise Burgers on Garlic Rolls

YIELD

4 servings

Per serving (with onion)
calories 754, protein 45 g,
fat 46 g, sodium 2043 mg,
carbohydrates 37 g,
potassium 612 mg

TIME

15 minutes preparation
15 minutes grilling

INGREDIENTS

2 pounds ground chuck
2 teaspoons salt
1/4 teaspoon pepper
1/2 teaspoon each marjoram and sage
4 Kaiser rolls
1/4 cup butter or margarine
1 clove garlic, minced
1/2 teaspoon onion salt
1/3 cup catsup
1 tablespoon white prepared
    horseradish

FILLINGS

4 thin slices onion; or 4 small slices
    cheese (cheddar, swiss, or blue); or
    8 green or black olives, sliced; or
    1/2 cup well-drained sauerkraut

Mix chuck, salt, pepper, marjoram, and sage. Cut meat into 8 pieces and shape each piece into a round burger about ½ inch thick ①.

Top 4 of the burgers with the desired filling ②. Cover with remaining burgers and pinch edges together ③.

Place burgers 6 inches above gray coals and grill for 5 to 6 minutes on each side.

Split the Kaiser rolls and place cut side down on grill rack. Grill for 2 minutes.

Melt the butter and stir in the garlic and onion salt. Turn the rolls and brush toasted side with garlic butter. Toast rolls another 2 minutes and brush other side with butter.

Place burgers on bottom of rolls. Mix catsup and horseradish and spoon on burgers. Replace top of roll. Serve at once with celery hearts, carrot sticks, radishes, and green pepper rings.

Speedy Chili Con Carne

YIELD

4 to 6 servings

Per serving (4)
calories 748, protein 38 g,
fat 43 g, sodium 1669 mg,
carbohydrates 54 g,
potassium 1496 mg

TIME

5 minutes preparation
45 minutes cooking

INGREDIENTS

1 tablespoon lard
½ cup chopped onion
1 pound ground beef
2 cups tomato sauce
1 clove garlic
1 teaspoon salt
1 tablespoon each ground pure hot
    and mild red chile
½ teaspoon ground cumino (cumin)

¼ teaspoon ground Mexican oregano
2 cups stewed pinto beans (Recipe 4)

Heat lard in a large saucepan, then add the onion and beef ①; cook until meat is lightly browned.

Add tomato sauce ② and simmer for 5 minutes. Add garlic, salt, ground chiles, *cumino*, and oregano; simmer for 30 minutes. Add pinto beans ③ and simmer for 10 more minutes. Taste and adjust seasoning. Ladle chile into soup bowls and serve.

Middle Eastern Pizza

YIELD

4 to 5 servings

Per serving (4)
calories 939, protein 40 g,
fat 39 g, sodium 1046 mg,
carbohydrates 108 g,
potassium 896 mg

TIME

1½ hours preparation
30 minutes cooking

INGREDIENTS

1 teaspoon honey
1¼ cups warm water
1 package active dry yeast
2½ cups all-purpose flour
1 cup whole-wheat flour
1 teaspoon salt
3 tablespoons olive oil

2 teaspoons ground cumin
Freshly ground black pepper to taste
¼ cup tomato paste
1 cup water
⅓ cup raisins
⅓ cup pinenuts (pignoli) or walnuts
⅓ cup sliced pimiento-stuffed green
    olives

FILLING

1 pound ground beef
1 onion, chopped
1 teaspoon ground cloves

GLAZE

1 egg white
1 tablespoon water

Dissolve honey in ¼ cup warm water and then add the yeast. Set aside until yeast foams.

Mix flours and salt, then add yeast mixture, remaining water, and oil. Turn out onto a floured board and knead until dough is smooth, about 5 minutes. Place dough in an oiled bowl, turning dough so that top of dough is lightly covered with oil. Cover with towel and let rise in a warm place until doubled in bulk, about 1 hour.

Brown meat in a skillet with the onion. Spoon off grease ①, then add cloves, cumin, pepper, tomato paste, water, and raisins. Simmer until water boils off and mixture is almost dry. Stir in nuts and olives and set aside.

Grease a 10-inch deep-dish pizza pan or baking dish. When dough has risen, punch down and divide into 2 parts. Using two-thirds of the dough, form a bottom crust by pressing into bottom and up sides of pan ②. To shape top crust, invert a 9-inch pie pan, grease the bottom, and pat dough onto pan to make a 10-inch round. Set aside.

Preheat oven to 400 degrees. Mound the filling into the dough-lined pan, allowing 1 inch of dough around the outside edge to remain uncovered. Top with the remaining dough and pinch the edges shut. Make a few slashes in top to allow steam to escape.

Mix egg white and water together for the glaze. Brush onto pastry top ③ and bake 30 minutes or until pizza is golden.

Liver Venetian Style

YIELD

4 servings

Per serving
calories 245, protein 17 g,
fat 17 g, sodium 260 mg,
carbohydrates 6 g,
potassium 308 mg

TIME

15 minutes preparation
10 minutes cooking

INGREDIENTS

¾ pound calves liver, or young steer
    liver, sliced very thin
2 tablespoons butter
2 tablespoons oil
1 large Spanish onion, sliced paper
    thin
Salt and pepper to taste
⅓ cup chicken broth, canned or fresh

Trim liver and remove all gristle or skin ①; cut into thin strips ②. In a skillet, heat butter and oil. Sauté onion slices over medium heat until soft and light golden—do not let brown. Remove onion to a plate and keep warm. Increase the heat under the skillet, and add liver slices. Sauté, shaking the pan a few times to prevent sticking, until liver is browned. This should take not longer than 2 minutes: the faster the liver is cooked, the tenderer it will be.

Return onion to skillet. Mix and heat through for half a minute, then season with salt and pepper. Remove liver and onions to a serving dish. Add broth to pan. Stir quickly to scrape up particles in pan and make a sauce. Spoon gravy over liver ③ and serve.

Oxtail Ragout

YIELD

4 servings

Per serving
calories 796, protein 24 g,
fat 62 g, sodium 1802 mg,
carbohydrates 37 g, potassium
771 mg

TIME

30 minutes preparation
2½ to 3 hours cooking

INGREDIENTS

⅔ cup all-purpose flour
2 teaspoons salt
½ teaspoon freshly ground pepper
2 pounds oxtails, cut up
4 tablespoons bacon fat, butter, or
    vegetable oil
½ cup chopped onion
½ cup diced carrots
1 small sweet red pepper, diced
1 stalk celery (no leaves), diced
1 clove garlic, crushed
1 bay leaf

½ teaspoon crumbled dried thyme
2 strips orange peel
1 cup tomato juice
2 cups beef broth
1 cup water
12 small yellow onions, peeled
½ pound mushrooms, sliced
3 tablespoons chopped fresh parsley

BEURRE MANIE

2 tablespoons butter
2 tablespoons flour

Preheat oven to 350 degrees.

Combine flour, salt, and pepper in a brown paper sack, then place a few pieces of oxtail at a time into the sack. Shake to coat with seasoned flour.

Melt the fat in a skillet and brown the oxtails on all sides. Transfer to an oven-proof casserole. In same fat, lightly brown the onion, carrots, pepper, and celery. Stir in garlic, bay leaf, thyme, and orange peel. Add these vegetables and spices to the casserole.

Add the tomato juice, beef broth, and water to the skillet and stir, cooking for a few seconds, to combine and pick up any particles stuck to the bottom of the skillet ①. Turn off the heat and pour the liquid over the oxtails.

Cover the casserole and place in oven. Cook for 2 hours, then add the small onions and cook another 30 to 45 minutes. Check and if oxtails are nearly done, add the mushrooms and cook covered for another 30 minutes.

Roll the butter with the flour into pea-sized balls ②. Remove ragout to stovetop and turn heat to low. Stir in the balls of butter and flour (*beurre manie*) and thicken the ragout ③. Top with parsley.

Veal Paprika

YIELD

4 servings

Per serving
calories 525, protein 45 g,
fat 30 g, sodium 668 mg,
carbohydrates 12 g, potassium
759 mg

TIME

20 minutes preparation
50 to 60 minutes cooking

INGREDIENTS

3 tablespoons butter
2 large red onions, thinly sliced
2 pounds veal shoulder, trimmed and
   cut in 1-inch cubes
Salt
1 heaping tablespoon + ½ teaspoon
   Hungarian sweet paprika
4 tablespoons tomato paste

½ teaspoon caraway seeds
½ cup dry white or red wine
1½ cups chicken stock
1 tablespoon warm water

Heat 2 tablespoons of butter in a heavy kettle. Add the onions and cook slowly to soften but do not brown. Add the veal and cook both veal and onions until delicately browned all over, turning now and then. Add salt to taste. Mix in 1 heaping tablespoon of paprika. Toss with meat and onions.

Add tomato paste and caraway seeds and blend well ①. Add the wine, stock, and enough water (if necessary) to cover the veal. Bring to a boil, reduce to simmer, cover, and cook slowly for 50 to 60 minutes or until meat is tender.

In a small saucepan, melt the remaining butter, add the remaining paprika and warm water, and blend ②. Stir this mixture into the veal. It gives the beautiful red sheen and characteristic Hungarian flavor. Serve with boiled potatoes or noodles.

Philadelphia Pepper Pot

YIELD

4 to 6 servings

Per serving (4)
calories 447, protein 42 g,
fat 18 g, sodium 1599 mg,
carbohydrates 28 g,
potassium 1035 mg

TIME

30 minutes preparation
3 hours cooking

INGREDIENTS

1 pound honeycomb tripe, diced
1 veal shank, in 2 pieces
1 quart chicken broth
1 clove garlic, mashed
1/4 teaspoon each dried thyme,
   marjoram, basil, savory
1 teaspoon salt
4 peppercorns
3 tablespoons butter or margarine
2 onions, chopped

2 stalks celery, chopped
2 green peppers, finely chopped
3 tablespoons all-purpose flour
2 large potatoes, peeled and diced

In a large kettle, combine tripe, veal, chicken broth, and about 1 quart water to cover completely. Bring to a boil, removing scum ①. Reduce heat; add garlic, herbs, salt, and peppercorns. Simmer 2 hours or until tripe is tender.

Remove tripe and veal, cutting veal pieces from bone into dice ②. Strain liquid ③ and reserve.

Melt butter in a large kettle, add vegetables, and cook over low heat until soft. Add flour, stir well, then add reserved liquid and cook over moderate heat until mixture thickens. Add meat and potatoes, reduce heat to low, and simmer 1 hour.

PORK AND LAMB

Pork Roast with Sausage Apple Stuffing

YIELD

10 or 12 servings

Per serving (10)
calories 881, protein 58 g,
fat 68 g, sodium 589 mg,
carbohydrates 6 g,
potassium 944 mg

TIME

45 minutes preparation
3 hours cooking

INGREDIENTS

3 tablespoons butter
¾ cup chopped onions
¼ cup chopped celery
½ cup peeled and chopped tart
   apples
½ cup bread crumbs
1 pound ground pork
½ pound well-seasoned sausage meat
½ cup finely chopped fresh parsley

½ teaspoon powdered sage
1 teaspoon salt
Freshly ground black pepper
1 crown roast, about 8 to 9 pounds

Preheat the oven to 350 degrees.

Melt butter and add onions, celery, and apples. Cook until soft. Add crumbs, then add ground pork, sausage, and seasonings; mix thoroughly.

Fill center of crown roast with stuffing, mounding center slightly ①. Cover with foil ② and wrap bone ends with additional foil ③. Roast in hot oven for 3 hours or until meat thermometer reads 175 degrees. About 30 minutes before roast is done, remove foil from stuffing.

Transfer roast to a large heated platter and remove foil. Add frills, if desired, and rest meat about 10 minutes before carving. Decorate roast on platter with a round of small potatoes, large mushrooms, or cooked red cabbage, if desired.

Roast Loin of Pork

YIELD

6 servings

Per serving
calories 530, protein 46 g,
fat 28 g, sodium 964 mg,
carbohydrates 19 g,
potassium 861 mg

TIME

20 minutes preparation
1 hour, 45 minutes
   cooking

INGREDIENTS

4 pounds lean loin of pork
¼ cup all-purpose flour
1 tablespoon oil
1 large clove garlic, crushed
1 teaspoon salt
Black pepper to taste
2 tablespoons soy sauce
½ teaspoon powdered ginger
1½ tablespoons lime juice
3 pineapple rings, cut in half
3 tablespoons brown sugar

BASTING SAUCE

½ cup pineapple juice
3 tablespoons cider vinegar

Remove most fat from the meat; sprinkle lightly with flour ①. Heat oil in a large skillet or roasting pan, and brown pork quickly on all sides. Remove from pan and cool slightly.

Preheat the oven to 350 degrees.

Combine garlic, salt, pepper, soy sauce, ginger, and lime juice; rub mixture into the roast ②. Place meat in a roasting pan, rib side down, cook in hot oven for 25 minutes per pound, or about 1 hour, 45 minutes. About 30 minutes before roast is done, place pineapple rings on top ③, sprinkle with sugar, and finish cooking.

During cooking, baste roast a few times with the pineapple juice–vinegar mixture and the pan juices. Serve with pan gravy.

Bourbon-Glazed Fresh Ham

YIELD

10 to 12 servings

Per serving (10)
calories 1124, protein 61 g,
fat 80 g, sodium 300 mg,
carbohydrates 24 g,
potassium 786 mg

TIME

30 minutes preparation
5 hours grilling

INGREDIENTS

1 fresh ham, about 10 pounds
1 cup bourbon
1 cup firmly packed brown sugar
½ teaspoon ground cloves
Grated rind of 1 orange
⅓ cup steak sauce

Trim rind from ham and score fat into diamonds ①.

Mix remaining ingredients in a bowl.

Tie ham every 2 inches with string ②. Spear ham on rotisserie rod and fasten ends. If desired, insert a meat thermometer in the center of the thickest part of the ham not touching a bone.

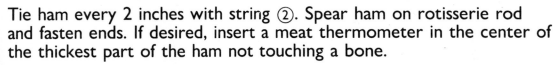

Make a drip pan ③ and place it in grill and arrange coals around it. Place ham 8 inches above gray coals and grill for 4 to 5 hours, adding more coals when needed.

During the last hour of grilling, brush glaze over all sides of ham. Brush with glaze every 10 minutes. Remove from rod and cut into thin slices. Serve with hot sauerkraut, skillet hash browns, and a pickled beet salad with caraway seeds.

NOTE *If using a meat thermometer, allow the ham to cook until it registers 170°F. This ham can also be roasted very successfully in a dome-type covered grill. See manufacturer's instructions for directions.*

Braised Pork Chops with Apples

YIELD

Serves 6

Per serving
calories 694, protein 32 g,
fat 58 g, sodium 312 mg,
carbohydrates 9 g,
potassium 619 mg

TIME

20 minutes preparation
40 minutes cooking

INGREDIENTS

6 pork loin chops
3 tablespoons butter
1 onion, thickly sliced
1 red eating apple, cored and sliced
   (skin on)
1½ tablespoons flour
½ cup apple juice or cider
½ cup chicken stock
Salt and freshly ground black pepper
   to taste

½ cup heavy cream
Handful of fresh parsley sprigs, finely
   chopped

Set the oven at 350 degrees. Slash the fat side of the pork chops so they don't curl during cooking ①. Melt the butter in a flameproof casserole and brown the pork chops a few at a time. Remove them from the pan, lower the heat, and cook the onion for a few minutes or until it begins to soften. Add the apple slices and sprinkle the flour into the pan ②. Cook, scraping the bottom constantly, until the flour is browned. At once pour in the apple juice or cider and the stock ③ and cook, stirring, until the sauce comes to a boil.

Replace the pork chops, turn them in the sauce, add salt and pepper to taste, cover, and cook in the preheated oven for 20 minutes, turning them over halfway through cooking.

Arrange the chops on a platter, cover with foil, and keep warm. Strain the cooking liquid into a saucepan and bring to a rolling boil. Skim the surface thoroughly, then pour in the cream and let the mixture bubble constantly for 2 minutes. Taste the sauce for seasoning, add more salt and pepper if necessary, and pour the sauce over the pork chops. Sprinkle some chopped parsley in a band down the center of the dish and serve with plain boiled rice.

Sweet and Sour Spareribs

YIELD

8 servings

Per serving
calories 1089, protein 39 g,
fat 79 g, sodium 1346 mg,
carbohydrates 54 g,
potassium 731 mg

TIME

10 minutes preparation
1 hour grilling

INGREDIENTS

8 pounds pork spareribs
Salt and pepper
½ green bell pepper
⅓ cup corn oil
2 teaspoons salt
3 cloves garlic, minced
2 cans (6 ounces each) frozen
   pineapple juice concentrate
1 cup firmly packed light brown sugar
1½ cups red wine vinegar
¼ cup soy sauce

Trim excess fat from the underside of the ribs ①. Cut into 2 rib sections ②, then sprinkle pieces with salt and pepper.

Mince the green pepper so you have ⅓ cup ③. Combine with remaining ingredients in a saucepan and place on grill. Simmer for 5 minutes.

Remove saucepan from the grill and place ribs on grill 8 inches above gray coals. Grill for 30 minutes, turning ribs every 10 minutes. Brush with sauce and grill for another 30 minutes, brushing and turning every 10 minutes.

Heat any remaining sauce and serve spooned over the ribs. Have plenty of napkins handy, as this is a sloppy, delicious dish. Serve with macaroni salad, grilled mushrooms, and foil-baked peas.

Santa Fe Spareribs

YIELD

4 servings

Per serving
calories 1023, protein 35 g,
fat 93 g, sodium 1152 mg,
carbohydrates 10 g,
potassium 886 mg

TIME

5 minutes preparation
3 hours marinating
2 hours baking

INGREDIENTS

2 pounds lean pork spareribs
6 cloves garlic, minced
1 teaspoon salt
¼ cup olive oil
Freshly ground black pepper
¼ cup red wine vinegar
½ teaspoon Mexican oregano
¼ cup minced onion
1 can (8 ounces) tomato sauce
1 cup Red Chile Sauce

Slice ribs into individual portions ① and place in oblong baking pan. Sprinkle with garlic, salt, oil, pepper, vinegar, oregano, and onion ②. Let stand for about 3 hours at room temperature.

Preheat oven to 350 degrees. Mix tomato sauce and chile sauce together and pour over the ribs ③. Place in oven and bake for 2 hours.

NOTE If in a hurry, the mixed tomato and chile sauce may be added after only 15 minutes of marinating. You can freeze up to 3 months, baked or unbaked.

Styrian Pork Casserole

YIELD

4 servings

Per serving
calories 582, protein 52 g,
fat 22 g, sodium 846 mg,
carbohydrates 42 g,
potassium 1998 mg

TIME

30 minutes preparation
1 hour, 15 minutes
cooking

INGREDIENTS

2 pounds lean pork (shoulder or butt)
2 tablespoons butter
2 medium onions, sliced thin
1 white turnip, pared and diced
2 large carrots, pared and diced
2 stalks celery (white part only), sliced
1 bay leaf
1 teaspoon dried marjoram

Pinch of dried thyme
1 teaspoon lemon juice
Salt and pepper to taste
2½ cups chicken broth
    (approximately), canned or fresh
4 large potatoes, peeled and diced

Trim most fat and any skin off the meat. Cut into 1½-inch cubes ①. In a heavy skillet, heat butter, and brown the pork. Remove from skillet and place in a saucepan ②.

Add onions, turnip, carrots, and celery to saucepan. Mix well, then add bay leaf, marjoram, thyme, and lemon juice; season with salt and pepper. Add enough chicken broth to barely cover the ingredients ③.

Bring to a boil over medium heat, cover, reduce heat, and simmer for about 45 minutes, until meat is nearly cooked. Add potatoes, and cook for another 15 minutes until potatoes are cooked.

Roast Pork with Shredded Vegetables

YIELD

4 to 6 servings

Per serving (4)
calories 395, protein 13 g,
fat 31 g, sodium 732 mg,
carbohydrates 12 g,
potassium 665 mg

TIME

25 to 30 minutes
preparation
4 to 5 minutes cooking

INGREDIENTS

8 dried black mushrooms
1 cup shredded Roast
  Pork
1 small red pepper
1 small green pepper
1 large piece bamboo shoot
1 large carrot
½ pound bean sprouts
4 scallions
1 piece gingerroot, about 3 inches
Oil for stir-frying

SAUCE

2 tablespoons thin soy sauce
1 tablespoon dry sherry
1 tablespoon oriental sesame oil
2 teaspoons red wine vinegar
2 teaspoons sugar

Soak the mushrooms in hot water to soften. Cut the pork into 3-inch shreds. Core and seed the peppers ①, then shred. Cut 6 thin lengthwise slices from the bamboo shoot ②; shred the slices into matchstick-sized pieces. Cut a 3-inch piece from the large end of the carrot, then peel and cut into thin slices; cut the slices into matchstick shreds ③. Rinse the sprouts, and drain and dry well. Wash and trim the scallions, then split in half and cut into 3-inch pieces.

Drain the mushrooms, squeeze dry, and remove and discard the stems; shred the caps. Peel the ginger and cut 3 thin lengthwise slices then cut into thin shreds. Put all the shredded ingredients on a large platter. Combine the sauce ingredients.

Heat a wok. Add 3 tablespoons oil, heat for 15 seconds, then add the pork, mushrooms, and peppers. Stir for 30 seconds. Remove to the work platter with a strainer. Add 2 tablespoons oil, heat for 10 seconds, then add the ginger and carrot. Stir for 30 seconds, add the bamboo, stir another 30 seconds, and then add the bean sprouts and scallions. Put the pork back in, along with the peppers and mushrooms. Stir to mix well. Stir the sauce and pour down the sides of the wok. Mix well, remove to a platter, and serve immediately.

Bremen Baked Ham

YIELD

4 servings

Per serving
calories 484, protein 40 g,
fat 24 g, sodium 2991 mg,
carbohydrates 21 g
potassium 794 mg

TIME

15 minutes preparation
30 minutes cooking

INGREDIENTS

½ cup dry red wine
¼ cup port wine
3 tablespoons red currant jelly
1 teaspoon dry mustard
1 teaspoon lemon juice
2 teaspoons cornstarch
1 ham steak, about 2 pounds

In a small saucepan, blend all ingredients except ham, and cook, stirring, over low heat until the sauce is clear and thickened ①.

Preheat oven to 325 degrees.

Place ham on a rack in a baking pan ②, then coat both sides with the sauce. Bake in hot oven for 30 minutes. Brush with sauce several times during cooking ③. When done, spoon remaining sauce over ham and serve.

Southern Stuffed Ham

YIELD

20 to 30 servings

Per serving (25)
calories 619, protein 44 g,
fat 47 g, sodium 1626 mg,
carbohydrates 1 g,
potassium 575 mg

TIME

Overnight soaking
45 minutes preparation
3 to 4 hours cooking
2 hours cooling

INGREDIENTS

1 country ham, about 12 to 16
  pounds
3 tablespoons butter
¼ cup finely chopped scallions (white
  and green parts)
½ cup finely chopped celery
½ pound fresh mustard greens,
  chopped
½ pound fresh spinach, chopped
1 teaspoon dried hot red pepper
  (optional)

½ teaspoon salt
Freshly ground black pepper

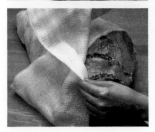

A day ahead place ham in a large kettle, cover with cold water, and soak at room temperature for 12 hours. Drain, add fresh water to cover, bring to boil over high heat, reduce heat, and simmer 1 hour. Remove from water, then cut off rind and excess fat, leaving no more than ⅛ inch fat.

In a heavy saucepan, melt butter, add scallions and celery, and cook about 5 minutes until soft. Stir in chopped greens and seasonings. Cook over low heat, covered, for about 7 to 10 minutes until soft.

To stuff ham, make 6 to 8 incisions 2 inches long and about 3 inches apart ①. Hold each incision open with a spoon and fill evenly with mixture ②. Wrap stuffed ham in cheesecloth ③; sew or tie securely.

Place ham in a large pot and cover with water. Bring to boil, then reduce heat to low, and simmer 3 to 4 hours, allowing about 15 minutes per pound, until ham is tender when pierced with knife point. Add water to keep ham covered when cooking, if necessary.

Remove ham to large platter and cool at room temperature for 2 hours, without removing cheesecloth. Just before serving, remove cheesecloth and carve in thin slices.

Roast Lamb with Eggplant

YIELD

Serves 4

Per serving
calories 911, protein 86 g,
fat 48 g, sodium 375 mg,
carbohydrates 32 g,
potassium 2088 mg

TIME

30 minutes preparation
45 minutes cooking

INGREDIENTS

5 pounds sirloin half of a leg of lamb,
   boned at the market
1/2 cup olive oil
1 tablespoon dried rosemary
Salt and freshly ground black pepper
   to taste
2 cloves garlic, cut in slivers
2 large eggplant, cut in large cubes
2 large onions, thinly sliced
3 green peppers, cut in strips

1 tablespoon tomato paste
1/4 cup chicken stock
1 pint cherry tomatoes, stems
   removed
Handful of parsley sprigs, finely
   chopped

Set the oven at 425 degrees. Tie the meat several times so it stays compact. Rub the fat side with 1 tablespoon of the olive oil and sprinkle it with rosemary, salt, and pepper. Insert the garlic slivers all over the meat ① and set it in a roasting pan. Roast the meat for 45 minutes for rare lamb, 55 minutes for medium and 65 minutes for well done. Rare lamb registers 130 degrees on a meat thermometer; medium registers 140 degrees; well done registers 160 degrees.

Meanwhile, sprinkle salt over the eggplant ② and set it in a colander placed over a deep plate ③. Let it sit for 15 minutes, then rinse and dry with a clean kitchen towel.

Heat 3 tablespoons of the remaining oil in a large skillet and add the eggplant. Stir constantly over a high heat until there is no more oil in the bottom of the pan. Remove the eggplant. Add the remaining 1/4 cup oil and cook the onions over a low heat until they are soft but not brown. Add the peppers with the tomato paste and stock and return the eggplant to the pan. Cover and cook over a medium-high heat for 20 minutes, stirring once or twice, until the eggplant is tender. Add black pepper to taste and stir in the cherry tomatoes.

Remove the strings from the lamb and carve it into thick slices. Arrange these on a platter and spoon the eggplant garnish beside it. Sprinkle the eggplant with parsley and serve at once.

Greek Grilled Leg of Lamb

YIELD

6 servings

Per serving
calories 743, protein 58 g,
fat 52 g, sodium 860 mg,
carbohydrates 2 g,
potassium 700 mg

TIME

15 minutes preparation
Overnight marinating
45 minutes grilling

INGREDIENTS

1 leg of lamb, about 5 to 6 pounds
1 cup olive oil
1 cup dry white wine
1 teaspoon each thyme and oregano
2 teaspoons salt
½ teaspoon pepper
½ teaspoon rosemary
2 cloves garlic, minced
2 teaspoons chopped mint leaves

Bone the leg of lamb ①, or have your butcher do it for you. Pound lamb until it is an even thickness ②. Place lamb in a shallow glass dish.

Mix remaining ingredients until well blended and pour over lamb ③. Turn meat in marinade, cover, and marinate in refrigerator overnight.

Drain lamb and reserve marinade. Place meat on grill 6 inches above gray coals and grill for 40 to 45 minutes, brushing with marinade and turning every 10 minutes.

Cut meat into thin slices (lamb will be pink) and sprinkle with chopped fresh mint. Serve with buttered noodles mixed with chopped olives and parsley and foil-baked carrots and oranges.

Rack of Lamb with Tiny Potatoes

YIELD

Serves 2

Per serving
calories 701, protein 51 g,
fat 37 g, sodium 242 mg,
carbohydrates 38 g,
potassium 1436 mg

TIME

30 minutes preparation
30 minutes cooking

INGREDIENTS

1 rack of baby lamb, trimmed of all
   its fat
1 tablespoon butter, at room
   temperature
Salt and freshly ground black pepper
   to taste
3 large all-purpose potatoes
2 tablespoons peanut oil
Bunch of watercress for garnish

Set the rack of lamb on a broiler pan and rub the fat side with butter. Sprinkle with salt and pepper and wrap the exposed bones with foil ①. Set aside for 10 minutes. Preheat the broiler.

Peel the potatoes and use a melon baller to scoop out rounds, cutting them as close together as possible to avoid wasting too much potato ②. (Cut up and use the scraps for making hash-browns.) Pile the balls into a saucepan and add cold water to cover. Bring to a boil and cook 1 minute. Drain and set aside until the lamb is half cooked.

Broil the lamb for 8 minutes on a side, setting it as close to the element as possible. This will give medium-rare lamb. Remove from the oven and let it sit in a warm place for 5 minutes more. (For medium-done lamb, broil it 11 minutes on a side; for well-done lamb, broil it 14 minutes on a side; in any case, let the meat rest after cooking for 5 minutes.)

Meanwhile, heat the peanut oil until it is quite hot, add the potatoes, and sauté them over a high heat ③, shaking the pan often, for 8 to 10 minutes or until they are tender and brown. Sprinkle with salt and pepper.

Carve the lamb and arrange 4 slices on each of 2 plates, crossing the exposed bones like swords. Arrange the potatoes on the plate and garnish with the watercress.

Jamaican Lamb Chops

YIELD

4 servings

Per serving
calories 229, protein 22 g,
fat 5 g, sodium 186 mg,
carbohydrates 17 g,
potassium 597 mg

TIME

10 minutes preparation
30 minutes cooking

INGREDIENTS

4 loin lamb chops, each ³/₄ inch thick,
   trimmed
²/₃ cup sliced red onions
²/₃ cup beef broth
¹/₃ cup port or madeira wine
²/₃ cup dried apricots or peaches
1 tablespoon grated gingerroot or
   ¹/₂ teaspoon ground ginger
2 teaspoons instant coffee powder
Salt and pepper
1 teaspoon cornstarch (optional)
Lemon or lime slices

In a large skillet, brown the meat with the onions ①. If meat is very lean, you may have to add a little oil.

Meanwhile, in a saucepan, heat the broth and wine and then add the dried fruit, ginger, and coffee ②, stirring to dissolve the instant coffee. Pour the liquid over the meat ③ and simmer, covered, for 15 to 20 minutes. Turn frequently to mix ingredients well.

Taste sauce and season to taste with salt and pepper. Thicken cooking liquid with cornstarch if desired, and garnish with lemon or lime slices.

Lamb and Vegetable Curry

YIELD

4 servings

Per serving
(without garnishes)
calories 293, protein 28 g,
fat 14 g, sodium 352 mg,
carbohydrates 13 g,
potassium 1018 mg

TIME

15 minutes preparation
30 minutes cooking

INGREDIENTS

1 pound lean boneless lamb
2 teaspoons butter
1 teaspoon safflower oil
2–3 cloves garlic, minced or crushed
1 onion, chopped
½ teaspoon each ground cardamom,
   coriander, and turmeric
¼ teaspoon ground cinnamon
¼ teaspoon minced gingerroot
1–3 teaspoons curry powder, depending on
   taste
1 cup plain yogurt
1 cup chicken broth
1 stalk celery, sliced
½ pound fresh mushrooms, sliced
½ pound asparagus or broccoli, cut in
   1-inch lengths
Cooked bulgur or rice
⅓ cup shredded raw carrots

GARNISHES

Unsalted raw cashews
Raisins
Plain yogurt
Kefir cheese
Sliced scallions
Lime wedges

Cut lamb into 1-inch cubes ①. Set aside.

Heat butter and oil in a large skillet, and sauté garlic and onion for 3 minutes, stirring often. Add lamb and brown cubes on all sides ②.

Add spices, yogurt, broth, celery, and mushrooms to skillet and simmer, covered, for 15 minutes. Add asparagus or broccoli on top of mixture in skillet and steam for an additional 10 minutes ③.

Place curry on a bed of bulgur or rice. Garnish with shredded carrots and serve with condiments, if desired.

Doris' Lamb Marakesh

YIELD

6 to 8 servings

Per serving (8)
calories 823, protein 53 g,
fat 36 g, sodium 1329 mg,
carbohydrates 71 g, potassium
1541 mg

TIME

20 minutes preparation
1½ hours cooking

INGREDIENTS

1 cup dark raisins
½ cup sherry
4 pounds lean boneless lamb, in
   2-inch cubes
3 teaspoons salt
½ teaspoon freshly ground pepper
½ cup + 2 tablespoons olive oil
2 onions, chopped
3 cloves garlic, chopped
1 teaspoon cayenne
2 teaspoons turmeric

½ teaspoon ground cinnamon
2 cans (35 ounces each) whole
   tomatoes
1 pound vermicelli or couscous
3–4 tablespoons chopped fresh
   coriander

Soak raisins in sherry while doing the other steps ①.

Pat lamb dry with paper towels, then season with salt and pepper ②. Heat ½ cup oil in a heavy kettle over high heat. When the foam dies down, brown the lamb a few pieces at a time on all sides ③. Do not let lamb pieces touch or they will not brown evenly. Take care not to burn the meat; lower heat, if necessary.

When meat has all browned, turn heat to medium and add the onions and garlic. Cook until onions are soft and transparent. Add the cayenne, turmeric, cinnamon and tomatoes. Mix thoroughly, then add raisins and sherry and mix again. Bring the liquid to a boil and cover. Reduce the heat to simmer and cook slowly for 1 to 1½ hours or until lamb is tender.

Prepare the vermicelli or couscous according to package directions. Top with coriander and remaining oil and serve with the lamb.

Irish Lamb Stew

YIELD

6 servings

Per serving
calories 668, protein 26 g,
fat 54 g, sodium 301 mg,
carbohydrates 17 g,
potassium 871 mg

TIME

20 minutes preparation
1 hour, 15 minutes
cooking

INGREDIENTS

2 pounds stewing lamb, cut in 2-inch
cubes
2 tablespoons all-purpose flour
½ cup lamb fat, bacon drippings, or
lard
1 medium onion, chopped
1 clove garlic, peeled and chopped
6 small white onions, peeled
1 bunch small carrots, trimmed and
scraped

2 tomatoes, peeled, seeded, and
chopped
½ cup shelled lima beans
½ teaspoon salt
1 teaspoon dried marjoram
¼ cup chopped fresh parsley

Dredge meat in flour ①, then shake off excess. Heat fat in a Dutch oven or stew pot and add meat. Stir to coat meat with fat ② and cook until brown, about 15 minutes. Add remaining ingredients ③ except parsley. Simmer, covered, until meat is tender, about 1 hour.

Season stew to taste. Add parsley during last 10 minutes of cooking, and serve with boiled potatoes.

add corn & peas instead of tomatoes — also add bacon w/ bacon drippings to reduce gaminess of lamb —

Also good to add homeade noodles.

Kashmir Meat Loaf

YIELD

4 to 6 servings

Per serving (4)
calories 418, protein 39 g,
fat 23 g, sodium 275 mg,
carbohydrates 11 g,
potassium 630 mg

TIME

15 minutes preparation
1 hour resting
1 hour cooking

INGREDIENTS

1 pound lean ground lamb
¾ pound lean ground beef
2 thick slices white bread, soaked in
    milk and squeezed dry
⅓ cup grated onion
2 cloves garlic, minced
1 egg, lightly beaten
1½ teaspoons curry powder, or to
    taste
1 teaspoon caraway seeds

1½ teaspoons lemon juice
2 tablespoons chopped fresh parsley
1 tablespoon dillweed
Salt and pepper to taste

Blend all ingredients. Pack the mixture into a loaf pan ① and let stand for one hour before cooking.

Preheat the oven to 350 degrees.

Place the loaf pan in a larger pan ②, add water about 1 inch deep ③, and bake in hot oven for 1 hour. Let cooked loaf sit for 5 minutes before slicing.

VEGETABLES

Grilled Vegetables

YIELD

6 servings each

TIME

10–20 minutes preparation
10–50 minutes grilling

FOIL-BAKED CORN

Shuck 6 ears of corn and place each ear on a square of heavy-duty foil. Top corn with 6 tablespoons butter, 1½ teaspoons sugar, a sprinkling of curry powder, and some red pepper flakes. Shape foil into packets, seal, and place on grill 6 inches above gray coals. Grill for 10 to 15 minutes, turning packets every 5 minutes.

GRILLED SQUASH PARMESAN

Place 3 sliced zucchini, 2 diced tomatoes, ½ teaspoon oregano, ½ teaspoon salt, and 3 tablespoons grated Parmesan cheese on a large square of heavy-duty foil ①. Top with 3 tablespoons butter. Shape foil into packet, seal, and place 6 inches above gray coals. Grill 20 to 25 minutes, turning packet every 10 minutes.

CAULIFLOWER POLONAISE

Place 1 cauliflower (broken into flowerets), ½ cup salted peanuts, and ½ cup shredded sharp cheddar cheese on a large square of heavy-duty foil. Add ½ cup well-seasoned chicken broth. Seal foil into packet and place on grill 6 inches above gray coals. Grill for 20 to 25 minutes, turning packet every 10 minutes.

STUFFED MUSHROOMS

Stuff 24 mushroom caps with a mixture of 2 tablespoons butter, 2 teaspoons instant minced onion, 1 cup grated sharp cheddar cheese, ¼ cup bacon bits, ½ cup fresh bread crumbs, and 2 tablespoons chopped parsley. Place 4 mushrooms on each square of heavy-duty foil and seal foil into packets ②. Place on grill 6 inches above gray coals and grill for 12 to 15 minutes. Do not turn packets.

FRENCH-STYLE PEAS

Place 2 unwrapped packages of frozen peas on a large square of heavy-duty foil. Top with ¼ cup butter, 4 shredded lettuce leaves, ½ teaspoon sugar, and a light sprinkling of salt and pepper ③. Seal foil into packets and place on grill 8 inches above gray coals. Grill for 10 to 15 minutes, turning packet every 5 minutes.

MICKIES

Place scrubbed Idaho potatoes on grill 6 inches above gray coals and grill for 40 to 50 minutes, or until potatoes are easily pierced and skins are crusty and black. Turn potatoes every 5 minutes. Serve split open and topped with a mixture of 1 cup sour cream and 3 tablespoons chopped chives. (Sweet potatoes or yams may be baked in the same way, only topped with ½ cup apricot preserves mixed with ¼ cup melted butter.)

NOTE Recipe analyses not available for these recipes.

Stir-Fried Cornucopia

YIELD

4 to 6 servings

Per serving (4)
calories 179, protein 4 g,
fat 12 g, sodium 403 mg,
carbohydrates 17 g,
potassium 579 mg

TIME

20 to 25 minutes
    preparation
3 to 4 minutes cooking

INGREDIENTS

3 stalks celery
1 small yellow onion
2 large red bell peppers
3 stalks bok choy
1 small zucchini
20 snow peas
3–4 tablespoons oil

SAUCE

1 tablespoon thin soy sauce
1/2 teaspoon wine or cider vinegar
1 teaspoon dry sherry
1/2 teaspoon sugar

Wash, trim, and string celery. Peel onion, quarter, and separate into sections ①. Remove tops from peppers and discard seeds; cut peppers into 1½-inch strips. Trim the root end and most of the green leaves of the bok choy. Split the zucchini in half; set one half aside for another use. Cut the celery, peppers, bok choy, and zucchini on the bias into bite-sized pieces ②. Blanch the snow peas. Combine sauce ingredients.

Heat a wok. Add 3 tablespoons oil and heat for 30 seconds. Add celery and stir-fry 15 to 20 seconds. Add onions and stir 15 seconds. Add peppers, stir 15 seconds. Remove to a work platter with a strainer ③.

Add remaining oil if necessary and heat 10 seconds. Add bok choy and zucchini, and stir 15 seconds. Put the celery, onions, and peppers back in wok, then add the snow peas. Stir sauce, and pour down the sides of the wok. Stir to mix well, remove to a platter, and serve immediately.

VARIATION *Top with lightly toasted sesame seeds or top with 1 to 2 teaspoons oriental sesame oil.*

NOTE *Proportions given for vegetables are suggestions. You may feature or diminish the role of any as desired.*

Pasta with Provencal Sauce

YIELD

4 servings

Per serving
calories 271, protein 8 g,
fat 2 g, sodium 483 mg,
carbohydrates 50 g,
potassium 419 mg

TIME

10 minutes preparation
25 minutes cooking

INGREDIENTS

2 red onions
2–3 zucchini
1 green pepper
1 tablespoon olive oil
3 cloves garlic, minced or crushed
1 can (16 ounces) whole tomatoes,
   drained
½ cup dry red wine
1–2 teaspoons chopped fresh basil
Salt
Freshly ground pepper
1 pound cooked pasta

Chop onions finely ①. Halve and then thinly slice the zucchini ②. Seed and core, then slice the green pepper ③.

Heat oil in large saucepan and sauté first onions, then zucchini and garlic until softened. Crush tomatoes and add, cooking briefly. Add remaining ingredients and simmer 15 minutes. Serve sauce over hot, drained pasta.

NOTE *This sauce also works well as an accompaniment to lamb or pork chops, or as a filling for an omelet.*

Asparagus or Broccoli Mimosa

YIELD

Serves 6

Per serving
(for asparagus)
calories 163, protein 4 g,
fat 13 g, sodium 108 mg,
carbohydrates 8 g,
potassium 435 mg

TIME

15 minutes preparation
30 minutes chilling
12 minutes cooking

INGREDIENTS

2 pounds fresh asparagus or 1 large
   head fresh broccoli
2 tablespoons white or red wine
   vinegar
1 teaspoon Dijon-style mustard
Salt and freshly ground black pepper
   to taste
Pinch of cayenne
1/3 cup olive oil
1 egg

Break off the asparagus ends where they snap naturally when you bend the spears ①. Trim the ends of the broccoli and use a small paring knife to peel the tough strings from each broccoli stem ②. Cut each stem into thin stalks ③. Cook either asparagus or broccoli in a skillet of boiling water for about 3 minutes for the asparagus and 5 minutes for the broccoli, or until they are both just done but still quite green. Drain into a roasting pan and fill the pan with very cold water and ice. Leave the vegetables to cool, then lift them from the water, arrange on a platter, blot dry with a clean towel, and cover tightly with plastic wrap.

Whisk the vinegar, mustard, salt, pepper, and cayenne together. Gradually whisk in the oil in a thin steady stream until the dressing emulsifies. Cover and set aside.

Prick a hole in the rounded end of the egg and gradually lower it into a pan of boiling water. When the water returns to the boil let the egg cook steadily for 12 minutes. Drain and plunge into a bowl of very cold water. When cool, peel and halve. Separate the yolk from the white.

To serve, pour the dressing over the vegetables on the platter and work the egg white through a sieve to make a band across the stems. Use the same sieve to work the yolk through, making a thinner band next to the white one. Serve at once.

Boston Baked Beans

YIELD

6 to 8 servings

Per serving (6)
calories 673, protein 21 g,
fat 18 g, sodium 692 mg,
carbohydrates 110 g,
potassium 1479 mg

TIME

Overnight soaking
45 minutes preparation
6 hours baking

INGREDIENTS

2 cups yellow-eye, navy, or small
  white beans
¼ pound salt pork, cut in half
1 small onion, peeled
1 to 2 teaspoons dry mustard
4 tablespoons molasses
3 tablespoons brown sugar

BROWN BREAD

½ cup seedless raisins
½ cup rye flour
½ cup yellow cornmeal
½ cup whole wheat flour
1 teaspoon baking soda
1 teaspoon salt
½ cup molasses
1 cup buttermilk

Soak beans overnight or 10 to 12 hours in water to cover. Bring to boiling point and simmer gently until skins burst, about 1 hour. Drain, saving water. Preheat the oven to 325 degrees.

Place 1 piece salt pork and the onion in the bottom of a 2-quart bean pot. Cover beans with 1 inch of water. Combine remaining ingredients with bean liquid and add to pot. Score remaining piece of salt pork with several gashes and place on top ①. Cover and bake about 6 hours. Do not stir while baking, but add water to keep beans covered. Remove cover for final hour so pork and beans will crisp. After 3 to 4 hours baking, taste to see if beans are sweet enough. If not, add more brown sugar or molasses. Serve with buttered slices of Boston Brown Bread.

While beans are baking, prepare brown bread. Soak raisins for 10 minutes in hot water to cover; drain and dry. Mix dry ingredients in a large bowl; add molasses and buttermilk. Mix well, then stir in raisins.

Butter thoroughly the inside and cover of a 1-pound coffee can or mold. Fill 2/3 full with batter, cover tightly ②, and set on a rack in a deep kettle ③. Add boiling water half way up sides of can. Cover kettle tightly and steam on top of stove for 2 hours, adding more water if necessary. Remove from mold and slice.

Harvard Beets

YIELD

4 servings

Per serving
calories 90, protein 1 g,
sodium 338 mg,
carbohydrates 22 g,
potassium 204 mg

TIME

5 minutes preparation
10 minutes cooking

INGREDIENTS

1 tablespoon cornstarch
¼ cup sugar
⅛ teaspoon black pepper
½ teaspoon salt
½ cup vinegar
¼ cup water or beet liquid
2 cups sliced, cooked beets or baby
   beets
1 tablespoon butter (optional)

In a saucepan, combine cornstarch, sugar, and seasonings. Add vinegar ① and water, bring to a boil over medium heat, and cook 5 minutes, stirring constantly.

Add beets to saucepan ② and heat thoroughly about 5 minutes or less. Just before serving, add butter ③ and mix well.

Fettuccine with Blue Cheese Sauce

YIELD

Serves 4

Per serving
calories 1291, protein 46 g,
fat 64 g, sodium 1456 mg,
carbohydrates 130 g,
potassium 550 mg

TIME

5 minutes preparation
5 minutes cooking

INGREDIENTS

1½ cups heavy cream
Freshly ground black pepper to taste
½ pound Roquefort, stilton or danish
    blue cheese, crumbled
2 cups broccoli flowerets
1½ pounds fresh fettuccine noodles
1 cup freshly grated parmesan cheese
    for serving

Bring a large stockpot of water to the boil for cooking the fettuccine.

Meanwhile in a heavy-based saucepan, combine the cream, pepper, and crumbled blue cheese and set over a low heat. Leave the sauce to heat gently, stirring occasionally, until it just reaches the boiling point.

Cut the broccoli flowerets into the smallest possible pieces ① and drop them into a saucepan of rapidly boiling water (not the water for cooking the fettuccine) ②. Cook 1 minute or until they are just done and still slightly crunchy, then drain ③ and set aside.

Cook the fettuccine in the rapidly boiling stockpot of water just until the noodles rise to the surface, about 2 minutes, or until they are tender but still have some bite.

Drain at once, shaking them in the colander, then divide the noodles among 4 dinner plates. Scatter some broccoli on each serving and divide the sauce among them. Serve at once, passing parmesan cheese separately.

Curried Carrots with Spaghetti Squash

YIELD

4 servings

Per serving
calories 135, protein 6 g,
fat 4 g, sodium 510 mg,
carbohydrates 18 g,
potassium 523 mg

TIME

10 minutes preparation
40 minutes cooking

INGREDIENTS

I small spaghetti squash
2 cups chicken or vegetable broth
I pound baby carrots, peeled
I tablespoon vermouth or dry white
   wine
I teaspoon curry powder
I teaspoon lemon juice
I teaspoon minced fresh parsley
3–4 tablespoons kefir or neufchatel
   cheese

Cut the squash in half and place face down on a steamer (if halves won't fit into your steamer, cut in quarters). Steam squash until tender, about 30 minutes, then using a fork, pull strands from the squash to have "spaghetti" ①. Keep warm on a shallow serving bowl or platter.

Bring the broth to a boil. Add the carrots and cook, covered, for 8 minutes or until just tender-crisp. Drain and reserve stock.

Combine 2 or 3 tablespoons of the stock with the vermouth, curry, lemon juice, parsley, and cheese. Add carrots ② and toss gently ③. Serve atop the squash and then garnish with additional minced parsley if desired.

Potato Cake

YIELD

4 servings

Per serving
calories 242, protein 6 g,
fat 11 g, sodium 257 mg,
carbohydrates 30 g,
potassium 720 mg

TIME

20 minutes preparation
2 hours chilling
30 minutes cooking

INGREDIENTS

1½ pounds white potatoes
2 tablespoons minced fresh parsley
1 clove garlic, crushed
Salt and pepper
2 tablespoons butter
1 tablespoon oil
⅓ cup grated Parmesan cheese

Scrub potatoes, place them in a saucepan, cover with cold water, bring to a boil, and simmer for 10 minutes. Drain and cool, then chill for 2 hours. Peel potatoes, then grate them coarsely into a bowl ①. Mix in parsley and garlic; season to taste with salt and pepper.

In a 7-inch nonstick skillet, heat butter and oil. Add potatoes, pack down ②, and smooth top and edges. Over medium heat, cook potatoes for about 7 minutes without stirring to brown the bottom. Shake the pan, and if you hear a rustling sound, the bottom is browned and crisp. Invert the cake onto a plate ③, then slide back into the skillet and brown the other side.

Slide the cake on a flameproof, flat serving dish. Sprinkle with grated cheese, then put under broiler to melt and lightly brown the cheese. Serve hot.

Thatched Potatoes in Cream

YIELD

Serves 4

Per serving
calories 506, protein 18 g,
fat 32 g, sodium 533 mg,
carbohydrates 36 g,
potassium 839 mg

TIME

15 minutes preparation
25 minutes cooking

INGREDIENTS

5 tablespoons butter
4 Idaho or Russet potatoes
3 tablespoons flour
2 teaspoons dry mustard
1¾ cups milk
Salt and freshly ground black pepper
   to taste
1½ cups grated cheddar cheese

Set the oven at 400 degrees. Use 2 tablespoons of the butter to grease 4 individual shallow baking dishes or gratin dishes.

Peel the potatoes and cut into thin slices. Cut across several slices at once to make matchstick pieces ①. Pile into a saucepan with cold water to cover, bring to a boil, and cook 2 minutes or until potatoes are almost tender.

Drain and shake to remove excess moisture. Divide between the 4 buttered dishes and set aside.

Melt the remaining butter in a saucepan and stir in the flour until smooth ②. Cook, whisking constantly for 1 minute. Gradually whisk in the mustard and milk ③ and stir constantly until the mixture comes to a boil. Lower the heat and let the sauce simmer for 2 minutes. Add salt and pepper to taste and pour the sauce over the potatoes. Sprinkle the cheese on top and bake the potatoes for 20 to 25 minutes or until they are crisp and brown. Serve at once.

Quick-Fried Spinach with Mushrooms

YIELD

4 to 6 servings

Per serving (4)
calories 90, protein 3 g,
fat 7 g, sodium 133 mg,
carbohydrates 5 g,
potassium 496 mg

TIME

*15 to 20 minutes
  preparation
2 to 3 minutes cooking*

INGREDIENTS

6 cups stemmed spinach leaves
12–16 fresh mushrooms
2 cloves garlic
2 tablespoons oil
⅛ teaspoon salt
Fresh black pepper

Rinse the spinach in the sink or a large bowl filled with cold water to remove sand ①. Pat or spin dry. Wipe mushrooms with a damp towel. Cut off stem ends but do not de-stem; cut into ¼-inch slices to yield 2 cups. Peel and slice garlic ②.

Heat a wok. Add the oil, heat 5 seconds, then add the garlic. Stir 10 seconds, then add the mushrooms and toss to coat with oil. Stir 10 seconds, then add the spinach. Press down with the spatula ③. Stir constantly, bringing the contents from the bottom to the top, coating the spinach with hot oil. Cook until the spinach has wilted but is not yet soggy. Sprinkle with the salt and pepper to taste. Mix well, then remove to a platter and serve immediately.

Acorn Squash with Apple Chutney

YIELD

8 servings

Per serving
calories 391, protein 6 g,
fat 10 g, sodium 93 mg,
carbohydrates 81 g,
potassium 1620 mg

TIME

30 minutes preparation
1 hour, 20 minutes
    cooking

INGREDIENTS

4 large acorn squash, cut in half and
    seeded
5 large green apples, peeled, cored,
    and cut in chunks
3 tablespoons butter, melted
3 tablespoons sugar
Juice of 2 lemons
1 large can (16 ounces) pineapple
    chunks, drained
1 teaspoon ground cinnamon

1/4 teaspoon ground nutmeg
1 cup cooked prunes
1 cup cooked apricots
3 tablespoons butter, diced

Preheat the oven to 350 degrees.

In 1 or 2 large baking dishes, place squash cut side down; add about 1½ cups water to each ①. Bake for 30 minutes. Turn oven temperature to 325 degrees.

In another baking dish combine apples and melted butter; bake 20 minutes.

In a mixing bowl, combine sugar, lemon juice, pineapple chunks, cinnamon, nutmeg, prunes, and apricots. Add apples.

Turn squash cut side up and fill halves with fruit mixture ②. Sprinkle with diced butter. Add liquid to a depth of ¼ inch ③. Bake for 30 minutes, or until squash is soft. Brown tops under the broiler if desired.

Julienne Vegetable Sauté

YIELD

Serves 6

Per serving
calories 148, protein 2 g,
fat 12 g, sodium 86 mg,
carbohydrates 10 g,
potassium 415 mg

TIME

30 minutes preparation
6 minutes cooking

INGREDIENTS

2 medium carrots
2 zucchini
2 yellow squash
2 red bell peppers, cored and seeded
5 tablespoons olive oil
Salt and freshly ground black pepper
  to taste
Handful of fresh mint leaves, finely
  chopped
Handful of fresh parsley sprigs, finely
  chopped

Halve the carrots lengthwise and cut each half on an extreme diagonal to make matchsticks ①. Put them into a saucepan with cold water to cover, bring to a boil, and cook steadily for 2 minutes. Drain and rinse with cold water; set aside.

Cut a thin lengthwise slice from each zucchini, then cut another lengthwise slice from the same side ②. Turn the zucchini on its flat side and cut 2 more lengthwise slices from another long side ③. Continue in this fashion with the third and fourth sides, until there is only a column of seeds left. (Add these seeds to soups.) Cut the slices on an extreme diagonal to make matchstick shapes. Cut the yellow squash in the same way.

Cut the red peppers into strips of the same size.

Heat the olive oil in a large skillet and add the zucchini, squash, and carrots. Cook over a medium-high heat, stirring often, for 3 minutes or until they are slightly softened. Add the red pepper strips and continue cooking for another 3 minutes or until all the vegetables are tender but still have some bite.

Add salt, pepper, mint, and parsley; stir to mix, and serve at once with broiled or grilled meats or fish.

Cherry Tomato and Basil Sauté

YIELD

Serves 4

Per serving
calories 84, protein 1 g,
fat 7 g, sodium 72 mg,
carbohydrates 4 g,
potassium 223 mg

TIME

5 minutes preparation
3 minutes cooking

INGREDIENTS

1½ pints cherry tomatoes, stems
  removed
2 tablespoons olive oil
2 cloves garlic, crushed
2 shallots, very finely chopped ①
Handful of fresh basil leaves, finely
  chopped ②
Salt and freshly ground black pepper
  to taste
Extra basil leaves for garnish

Have the cherry tomatoes sitting near the stove. Heat the olive oil in a large skillet and when it is quite hot, add the cherry tomatoes, garlic, and shallots. Cook over a medium-high heat, shaking the pan constantly ③, for 1 to 3 minutes or until the cherry tomatoes are tender but have not shriveled or burst.

Remove them from the pan and transfer to a serving dish. Sprinkle with basil, salt, and pepper and stir well to combine them. Garnish with extra basil leaves and serve at once.

SALADS

Chicory Salad with Anchovy Pastries

YIELD

4 servings

Per serving
calories 543, protein 12 g,
fat 44 g, sodium 699 mg,
carbohydrates 26 g,
potassium 338 mg

TIME

20 minutes preparation
25 minutes baking

INGREDIENTS

1 cup all-purpose flour
½ cup butter or margarine
Salt and pepper
2 cloves garlic, 1 chopped and 1
   crushed
2½ cans (2 ounces each) anchovy
   fillets, drained
3 tablespoons butter
1 egg, lightly beaten
1 head chicory
2 tablespoons oil
1 tablespoon vinegar

Preheat the oven to 350 degrees.

Prepare the pastry first by cutting the butter into the flour ①. Add a dash of salt and the chopped garlic. Season to taste with pepper. Knead lightly to form a smooth dough, then spread it onto a buttered baking sheet, making a rectangle about 12 by 15 inches.

Blend the anchovies with the 3 tablespoons butter until it is a smooth purée. Spread the purée over the pastry ②, to within ½ inch of the edges. Fold the pastry over ③ and press together lightly. Glaze pastry with beaten egg and bake for 25 minutes in moderate oven. When lightly brown and crisp, remove from oven and let cool. Cut into squares.

Wash the chicory and drain well. Break apart and place leaves into a salad bowl.

Prepare an oil and vinegar dressing, season with salt and pepper, and add the crushed clove of garlic. Toss the salad with the dressing just before serving, and accompany with anchovy pastries.

From *French Provincial Cuisine* by Christian Délu

Greek Salad with Cheese Pita Breads

YIELD

6 servings

Per serving
calories 657, protein 26 g,
fat 45 g, sodium 854 mg,
carbohydrates 40 g,
potassium 546 mg

TIME

20 minutes preparation
15 minutes cooking

INGREDIENTS

3 cups cubed iceberg lettuce
3 cups torn pieces romaine
1 cup radish slices
½ cup white onion rings
4 ounces crumbled feta cheese or
   farmer cheese
3 tomatoes, cut into wedges
1 can (2 ounces) anchovy fillets,
   drained
18 black or Greek olives
1 cucumber, cut into thin slices

½ cup olive oil
¼ cup red wine vinegar
½ teaspoon salt
¼ teaspoon pepper
½ teaspoon oregano
1 teaspoon sugar
6 pita breads
1 pound mozzarella cheese, shredded

In a large bowl, mix lettuce, romaine, radishes, onion rings, feta cheese, tomatoes, anchovies, olives, and cucumber ①. Cover and chill.

In a bowl, beat oil with vinegar, salt, pepper, oregano, and sugar until thick ②. Let stand at room temperature.

Slash pita breads at one side and stuff each with mozzarella cheese ③.

When almost ready to serve, preheat oven to 400 degrees. Place pita breads into hot oven for 15 minutes. Cool 5 minutes, then cut into quarters. Meanwhile, beat dressing again and pour over salad. Toss to coat all particles. Serve pita breads warm with dressed salad.

Insalata Mista Cotta e Cruda

YIELD

4 servings

Per serving
calories 338, protein 5 g,
fat 29 g, sodium 162 mg,
carbohydrates 20 g,
potassium 968 mg

TIME

10 minutes preparation
20 minutes cooking

INGREDIENTS

4 fresh zucchini, not longer than 4 to
   5 inches
4 large carrots, peeled
1 cup sliced young fresh green beans
1/2 pound fresh, young spinach leaves,
   washed and drained
Salt and freshly ground black pepper
2 tablespoons wine vinegar
1/2 cup olive oil

Wash the zucchini and scrape off any rough spots but don't peel. Bring water to a boil and add the whole zucchini. Boil for 5 to 6 minutes, according to size. If you can stick a fork in easily, they are done. Remove, let cool, and slice into pieces 1/3 inch thick.

Slice the carrots into pieces about the size of the zucchini, then cook in boiling water for 5 to 6 minutes until tender. Drain and let cool.

Cook the green beans in boiling water until tender, about 6 to 8 minutes. Drain and let cool.

Place the cooked vegetables in a salad bowl and add the spinach leaves. Stir to mix completely.

Place the desired amount of salt and pepper into a serving spoon. Fill the spoon with the vinegar, and with a fork stir to dissolve ① the salt in the spoon. Pour this over the salad.

Holding a cruet of oil a few inches above the bowl, pour a thin stream of olive oil over the salad ②. Taste and, if you want more sharpness, add more vinegar ③. The taste of these fresh young vegetables is so delicate that a little vinegar will go a long way. Mix very well and serve.

From *The Cuisine of Venice* by Hedy Giusti-Lanham and Andrea Dodi

Green Bean and Artichoke Salad with Goat Cheese

YIELD

8 servings

Per serving
calories 411, protein 8 g,
fat 32 g, sodium 283 mg,
carbohydrates 30 g,
potassium 675 mg

TIME

30 minutes preparation
25 minutes cooking
1 hour chilling

INGREDIENTS

32 walnut halves
1½ pounds tender green beans
2 tablespoons all-purpose flour
Juice of 1 lemon
8 artichokes
Bibb or Boston lettuce
Small goat banons or slices of Saint-
    Saviol Bucheron
Parsley and chives, chopped
Lavender-colored flower blossoms
    (violets, chives, borage, or hyssop
    blossoms)

DRESSING

⅓ cup red wine vinegar
Salt and pepper
⅓ cup olive oil
⅓ cup walnut oil
Minced herbs (parsley, chives)

Prepare a walnut-oil vinaigrette by adding salt and pepper to the vinegar and stirring until the salt dissolves. Stir in the oils and the herbs, and mix with a fork until well blended. Taste for seasoning.

Bring a small pot of water to a boil and plunge in the walnuts. Boil for 3 minutes, then drain and peel.

Cook the beans in salted boiling water until just tender. Drain and cool.

Bring a large pot of salted water to a boil. Mix the flour with ¼ cup of water and add the paste and lemon juice to the pot. Using a stainless-steel knife, cut off the artichoke stems ①, snap back the leaves, and cut off 1½ inches of each's top ②. Trim the artichokes of dark leaf portions until only the hearts remain ③. Cook in the boiling water until a knife point easily pierces the stem end. Strain from the water and lift off the choke portions.

Immediately add artichokes to the vinaigrette, turning them well in the oil; then add the beans and marinate at room temperature for at least 1 hour.

To serve, prepare a small bed of lettuce leaves on each plate. Place goat cheese portion in the middle, then swirl green beans around it. Garnish with artichokes, walnuts, herbs, and lavender flowers. Drizzle any remaining dressing over each portion.

From *Judith Olney's Entertainments*

Spinach and Feta Salad

YIELD

8 servings

Per serving
calories 240, protein 9 g,
fat 20 g, sodium 344 mg,
carbohydrates 8 g,
potassium 659 mg

TIME

10 minutes preparation

INGREDIENTS

2 pounds fresh spinach
½ cup olive oil
2 tablespoons white wine vinegar
2 tablespoons lemon juice
¼ teaspoon ground cinnamon
¼ teaspoon powdered mustard
Salt and pepper
2 cucumbers
4 hard-cooked eggs
¼ pound feta cheese, crumbled
2 green onions, chopped

Remove the stems from the spinach ①. Wash and drain leaves, then cut into 1-inch-wide strips ②. Put the spinach in a salad bowl.

Blend together the oil, vinegar, lemon juice, and spices. Pour half the dressing over the spinach and mix well.

Thinly slice the cucumbers (with or without peel) and arrange on top of the spinach. Slice the eggs and arrange on top of the cucumbers ③.

Sprinkle salad with cheese and onions. Pour remaining dressing over salad.

From *The Regional Cuisines of Greece* by The Recipe Club of St. Paul's Greek Orthodox Church

Old-Fashioned Potato Salad

YIELD

6 servings

Per serving (without garnish)
calories 452, protein 6 g, fat 30 g, sodium 348 mg, carbohydrates 42 g, potassium 1055 mg

TIME

20 minutes preparation
20 minutes cooking

INGREDIENTS

3 pounds new potatoes (about 7 medium)
½ cup chopped onion ①
½ cup chopped celery
½ cup chopped green pepper
¼ cup chopped fresh parsley ②
1 cup mayonnaise
Salt and pepper to taste
6 large lettuce leaves
2 hard-cooked eggs for garnish

Cook potatoes in boiling water and a pinch of salt until tender when pierced with a fork but not soft, about 20 minutes. Drain, then run under cold water. Peel, then slice or dice ③.

Combine vegetables with potatoes and bind with mayonnaise. Season with salt and pepper. Place lettuce leaves on a platter, add salad, and circle with slices or wedges of hard-cooked eggs.

Roasted Red Pepper Salad

YIELD

Serves 4

Per serving
calories 322, protein 2g,
fat 30 g, sodium 158 mg,
carbohydrates 13 g,
potassium 407 mg

TIME

10 minutes preparation
30 minutes chilling
15 minutes cooking

INGREDIENTS

6 large red bell peppers
½ cup top-quality olive oil
2 shallots, very finely chopped
Salt and freshly ground black pepper
   to taste
¼ cup imported black olives

Preheat the broiler. Set the peppers in a small roasting pan and rub them very lightly with olive oil, reserving the remaining oil for later. Broil the peppers as close to the element as possible, turning them every few minutes or as soon as they are charred on one side ①. When they are charred all over—this may take 15 minutes altogether—drop them into a large bowl of ice water and leave for a few minutes or until they are cold.

Remove the peppers from the water and work over a bowl to cut off the stem end, split each lengthwise in half, and discard the ribs and seeds ②. Peel off the charred skins ③ and arrange 3 halves on each of 4 salad plates.

Sprinkle the remaining oil on the peppers and decorate each plate with a thin band of chopped shallots running across the peppers. Wrap tightly and refrigerate 15 to 30 minutes or until cold.

Just before serving, sprinkle with salt and pepper and garnish each plate with black olives. Serve as an appetizer with thick slices of toasted Italian bread and butter.

Stuffed Tomatoes

YIELD

4 servings

Per serving
calories 96, protein 5 g,
fat 7 g, sodium 204 mg,
carbohydrates 5 g,
potassium 227 mg

TIME

15 minutes preparation

INGREDIENTS

2 firm tomatoes
⅓ cup diced cooked chicken breast
¼ cup heavy cream
1 tablespoon catsup
2 teaspoons chopped chives
Salt
Pinch of sweet paprika
3 stuffed green olives

Cut the tops off the tomatoes ①, and discard tops. Scoop out the flesh of the tomato and discard seeds ②; use pulp for another purpose. Lightly salt the insides of the tomatoes and turn upside down to drain briefly.

Mix the chicken, cream, catsup, and chives. Season to taste with salt and paprika, then spoon the mixture into the tomatoes ③. Serve garnished with sliced olives.

Crabmeat and Artichoke Salad

YIELD

4 servings

Per serving

calories 110, protein 8 g,
fat 6 g, sodium 658 mg,
carbohydrates 3 g,
potassium 185 mg

TIME

5 minutes preparation
2 hours chilling

INGREDIENTS

1 can (10 ounces) artichoke hearts
1 can (6 ounces) crab meat
1 can (2 ounces) sliced ripe olives
1 teaspoon grated lemon rind

LOW-CALORIE VINAIGRETTE

1/2 cup chicken broth
3 tablespoons vegetable oil
1/4 cup plus 1 tablespoon red wine
    vinegar or lemon juice
1 teaspoon dry or Dijon-style mustard
Salt and freshly ground pepper

Combine ingredients for dressing in a small bowl and blend with a wire whisk ①. This will make 1 cup of vinaigrette. For this recipe you'll need 1/4 cup; save the remainder for another use.

Drain the artichokes and crab meat ②. Combine artichokes, crab meat, olives, and lemon rind, then stir in 1/4 cup vinaigrette ③. Chill for 2 or more hours.

NOTE *If desired, add fresh minced parsley, chopped hard-cooked egg, or 1/2 teaspoon dried herb of your choice.*

Smoked Fish Salad

YIELD

4 servings

Per serving
calories 353, protein 33 g,
fat 16 g, sodium 5934 mg,
carbohydrates 20 g,
potassium 1120 mg

TIME

25 minutes preparation

INGREDIENTS

12 ounces smoked whitefish (or sable
   or sturgeon)
1 apple
3 tomatoes
4 ounces Gouda cheese
2 cups sliced celery
1 small head Boston lettuce

DRESSING

1 cup plain yogurt
2 tablespoons oil
1 tablespoon lemon juice
1/2 teaspoon black pepper
1/2 teaspoon salt
Pinch of sugar (optional)
2 tablespoons chopped chives

Remove the skin ① and bones from the fish. Flake it off the bones ②.

Peel and dice the apple. Dice the tomatoes and cheese. Wash and trim the lettuce. Tear it into bite-size pieces and place in a salad bowl.

Add the celery, fish, fruit, and cheese to the salad bowl.

Mix the yogurt with the remaining dressing ingredients ③ and toss with salad. Chill for only a short time before serving.

Chicken and Shrimp Salad

YIELD

6 servings

Per serving
calories 633, protein 36 g,
fat 39 g, sodium 675 mg,
carbohydrates 33 g,
potassium 709 mg

TIME

15 minutes preparation
1 hour chilling

INGREDIENTS

3 cups diced cooked chicken or turkey
1 pound shrimp, cooked, shelled, and
   deveined
3 cups cooked rice
1 cup chopped celery
½ cup sliced stuffed olives
3 ripe tomatoes, diced
1 green pepper, diced
Mayonnaise, about 1 cup
Juice of 1 lemon
Romaine lettuce leaves
2 hard-cooked eggs, chopped

In a large bowl, mix chicken, shrimp, rice, celery, olives, tomatoes, and pepper with enough mayonnaise to make a moist mixture ①. Stir in lemon juice. Chill.

When ready to serve, line a salad bowl with lettuce leaves ②. Add salad and top with eggs. Serve with cornbread squares spread with scallion butter.

NOTE Technique photo ③ shows an easy way to chop hard-cooked eggs or egg slices by cutting them first across their width, then reinserting into the slicer and cutting them lengthwise.

Chinese Tossed Chicken Salad

YIELD

6 servings

Per serving
calories 378, protein 17 g,
fat 28 g, sodium 861 mg,
carbohydrates 16 g,
potassium 348 mg

TIME

25 minutes preparation
10 minutes cooking

INGREDIENTS

1 small chicken, cooked and cooled
4 tablespoons sesame seeds
8 to 10 sprigs Chinese parsley
3 whole scallions
3 cups oil
2 ounces Chinese rice sticks
1 small head iceberg lettuce
Freshly ground black pepper

DRESSING

3 tablespoons lemon juice
1 1/2 tablespoons dry mustard
1 tablespoon water
1/4 cup peanut oil
1 tablespoon sesame oil
1 tablespoon granulated sugar
1 teaspoon chicken bouillon powder
2 tablespoons light soy sauce
1/2 teaspoon salt
1 clove garlic, minced

Skin and bone the chicken and tear the meat into julienne shreds. Reserve any juices from the chicken. Set aside.

Toast the sesame seeds in a small pan over medium heat until light brown ①, about 1 minute; do not allow to burn. Set aside.

Mix the ingredients for the dressing in a bottle and chill in refrigerator.

Clean the parsley and break the leaves from the stems. Discard the stems; you should have about 1 cup of leaves.

Trim and shred the scallions finely. Set aside.

Set a wok or deep skillet over high heat. When the wok is very hot, add the oil. Wait for about 10 minutes, then test the temperature by throwing a few inches of rice sticks into the oil. The temperature is hot enough if the rice sticks puff up immediately (about 400 degrees). Otherwise wait a little longer and test again.

When the oil is hot and smoke starts to appear on the surface, add about 1/4 of the rice sticks. They should puff up and cover the surface of the oil instantly. Turn them quickly ② and deep-fry the other side until puffy. Remove from oil quickly; you want the sticks creamy white, not brown. Finish frying the remaining rice sticks and keep all warm in a warm oven.

Shred the lettuce just before serving; you should have about 3 cups of greens. Combine the shredded lettuce and scallions, parsley leaves, shredded chicken, chicken juices, and sesame seeds in a large bowl. Add dressing and black pepper to taste and toss well. Spread rice sticks on top of salad and serve warm.

From *The Cuisine of China* by Pearl Chen, T.C. Chen, and Rose Tseng

Curried Tuna-Rice Salad

YIELD

6 servings

Per serving
calories 338, protein 13 g,
fat 18 g, sodium 900 mg,
carbohydrates 32 g,
potassium 500 mg

TIME

15 minutes preparation
20 minutes cooking
5–7 hours chilling

INGREDIENTS

2 cups water
3 chicken bouillon cubes
1 cup rice, uncooked
1 can (7 ounces) water-packed tuna
2 tablespoons vegetable oil
1/3 cup chopped scallions
2 teaspoons curry powder
3 tablespoons lemon juice
3 tablespoons vinegar
3 tablespoons olive oil
2 cloves garlic, finely minced

Lettuce leaves
1 avocado, peeled, seeded, and sliced
1 tomato, cut in wedges
Lemon slices and parsley for garnish
Condiments: chopped cucumber,
   sieved hard-cooked egg, chopped
   peanuts, crisp bacon bits

Place the water and chicken bouillon cubes in a medium saucepan. Bring to a boil and slowly add 1 cup rice. Cover and cook over low heat for 20 minutes. Cool slightly.

Drain and flake tuna. Combine with rice. Set aside.

In a skillet heat the vegetable oil and sauté scallions; remove and add curry powder to pan. Cook 1 minute, then blend in lemon juice, vinegar, olive oil, and garlic. Pour dressing over tuna-rice mixture. Mix in scallions and blend thoroughly ①.

Pack mixture into a round 1-quart mixing bowl or mold lined with plastic wrap ②. Refrigerate several hours to blend flavors.

Unmold onto lettuce-lined serving platter ③. Arrange avocado slices and tomato wedges around salad. Garnish with lemon slices and parsley. Serve with a selection of condiments such as cucumber, sieved egg, peanuts, and bacon bits.

Manhattan Beach Seafood Salad

YIELD

8 servings

Per serving
calories 428, protein 23 g,
fat 17 g, sodium 1695 mg,
carbohydrates 44 g,
potassium 274 mg

TIME

15 minutes preparation
4 minutes cooking
2 hours chilling

INGREDIENTS

4 quarts water
1 tablespoon each salt and oil
1 pound fresh pasta, preferably green
  or orange
½ pound cooked small shrimp
1 can (10 ounces) whole clams,
  drained
1 can (6 ounces) crab meat
1 red or green pepper, thinly sliced

1 small cucumber, peeled in alternate
  strips, then quartered and thinly
  sliced
¼ cup each capers, minced fresh
  parsley, and sliced ripe olives
½ cup kefir cheese
½ cup low-calorie vinaigrette
Green leaf lettuce

Bring water, salt, and oil to a boil in a large kettle. Add pasta and cook about 4 minutes, or until *al dente*. Rinse, drain ①, and place in large bowl.

Add the remaining ingredients except the cheese and the dressing. Mix gently. Whisk the cheese and vinaigrette together to form a creamy sauce ②, then pour onto salad, toss gently ③, and chill for a couple of hours.

To serve, place salad in a large bowl and surround with green leaf lettuce.

Oriental Beef Salad

YIELD

4 to 6 servings

TIME

15 minutes preparation
10 minutes cooking
1 hour chilling

INGREDIENTS

1 flank steak, about 1½ pounds
2 tablespoons oil
2 small chilies or 1 large, seeded and diced
1 clove garlic, minced
1 large yellow onion, sliced
3 scallions, green and white parts separated, chopped
½ pound fresh mushrooms, sliced
½ cup sliced waterchestnuts

1 large red onion, chopped
1 teaspoon minced gingerroot
1 tablespoon soy sauce
2 tablespoons water
1 tablespoon pale dry sherry
2 teaspoons rice vinegar
1 tablespoon chopped coriander or parsley
1 teaspoon chopped chives
Salt and freshly ground pepper

Remove all fat from the meat and cut into julienne pieces about ½ inch wide and 3 inches long ①.

Heat 1 tablespoon of the oil until very hot in a skillet and add the hot pepper. Stir around in the hot oil to flavor it, then discard the pepper. Add the garlic, sliced onion, and scallion whites to the skillet. Sauté very briefly, just until wilted. Transfer to a large bowl and then add the mushrooms to the skillet. Sauté until they absorb some of the oil and become brown but are still firm. Transfer to the bowl with the onion and scallions. Add the remaining tablespoon of oil and put in the meat strips. Stir-fry for about 5 minutes, or until the meat starts to brown lightly ②. Transfer the meat to the bowl, and add the water-chestnuts, red onion, and ginger.

In a small dish, combine the soy sauce, water, sherry, and vinegar. Swirl this into the skillet and cook briefly, scraping up the particles on the bottom of the pan. Blend well, then pour over the ingredients in the bowl ③. Sprinkle on the coriander and chives and top with the scallion greens. Chill for about 1 hour, taste for seasoning and add salt and pepper if desired.

NOTE Analysis not available for this recipe.

Salami-Green Bean Salad

YIELD

4 servings

Per serving
calories 461, protein 15 g,
fat 41 g, sodium 1284 mg,
carbohydrates 10 g,
potassium 361 mg

TIME

10 minutes preparation
1 hour chilling

INGREDIENTS

1 can (1 pound) cut green beans
8 ounces salami in 1 piece
2 medium onions

DRESSING

6 tablespoons oil
3 tablespoons vinegar
1 clove garlic, crushed
Salt and black pepper

Drain the beans. Cut the salami into thin strips ①. Thinly slice the onions ②. Mix all ingredients in a bowl.

Beat oil and vinegar with garlic. Season to taste with salt and pepper. Toss salad with dressing ③. Chill 1 hour before serving.

DESSERTS, CAKES, AND COOKIES

Zabaglione

YIELD

6 servings

Per serving
calories 127, protein 2 g,
fat 2 g, sodium 10 mg,
carbohydrates 24 g,
potassium 404 mg

TIME

10 minutes preparation

INGREDIENTS

2 egg yolks
3 tablespoons granulated sugar
1 teaspoon lemon juice
¼ cup marsala or madeira wine
1 cup blueberries
2 peaches, sliced
2 cups cantaloupe balls
3 cups hulled strawberries

In top of double boiler, beat egg yolks and sugar until combined. Place over double boiler filled with hot, not boiling water. Beat until frothy ①.

Add lemon juice. Continue to beat, adding marsala, 1 tablespoon at a time, until sauce is smooth and thick ②. Do not overcook.

Place fruit into individual serving dishes ③. Spoon zabaglione over fruit. Serve immediately.

Sautéed Apples in Custard Sauce

YIELD

Serves 6

Per serving
calories 337, protein 5 g,
fat 19 g, sodium 164 mg,
carbohydrates 37 g,
potassium 257 mg

TIME

20 minutes preparation
30 minutes chilling
10 minutes cooking

INGREDIENTS

4 large Granny Smith or other tart
    eating apples
6 tablespoons butter
¼ cup sugar

SAUCE

2 cups milk
5 egg yolks
¼ cup sugar
1 teaspoon vanilla extract
Extra sugar for sprinkling

For the sauce, scald the milk in a heavy-bottomed saucepan. Blend the yolks and sugar thoroughly in a bowl with a wooden spoon and gradually stir in the hot milk. Return the mixture to the saucepan and stir over low heat until it thickens to the consistency of heavy cream. Do not boil or it will curdle.

At once strain the mixture into a bowl ① and stir in the vanilla. Sprinkle the top with a very light coating of sugar and refrigerate the sauce for 30 minutes or until cold.

Pare the apples, quarter them, and remove the stems and cores. Halve the quarters to make 32 apple wedges ②. Melt the butter in a large skillet and when it is foaming, add the apple wedges. Cook over a high heat for half a minute, then turn them over and sprinkle with the sugar. Cook another few minutes or until the sugar begins to caramelize ③, then remove the pan from the heat.

Coat 6 dessert plates with some of the custard sauce and arrange 5 or 6 apple wedges, like the spokes of a wheel, on the sauce. Serve at once.

Chocolate Bread Pudding

YIELD

6 servings

Per serving
calories 370, protein 8 g,
fat 19 g, sodium 343 mg,
carbohydrates 44 g,
potassium 287 mg

TIME

15 minutes preparation
45 to 50 minutes cooking

INGREDIENTS

6 to 7 slices stale bread
2 eggs
¾ cup granulated sugar
⅓ cup unsweetened cocoa
1 teaspoon ground cinnamon
¾ teaspoon vanilla extract
¼ cup butter, melted
¼ teaspoon salt
2½ cups milk
⅓ cup heavy cream
1 tablespoon confectioners sugar

Preheat oven to 350 degrees. Grease a 9½-inch oval baking dish (5½ to 6 cups). Cut crusts off bread. Cut bread into ½- to ¾-inch cubes to make 5 cups ①.

In medium bowl, beat eggs, sugar, cocoa, cinnamon, and ½ teaspoon vanilla until blended. Beat in butter and salt. Gradually stir in milk ②. Add bread, stirring to break up cubes ③. Pour into dish. Bake 45 to 50 minutes, until a knife inserted in center comes out clean.

In small bowl, beat heavy cream, confectioners sugar, and remaining ¼ teaspoon vanilla until stiff. Serve over bread pudding.

Raspberries Romanoff

YIELD

Serves 6

Per serving
calories 306, protein 2 g,
fat 25 g, sodium 27 mg,
carbohydrates 18 g,
potassium 171 mg

TIME

15 minutes preparation
30 minutes chilling

INGREDIENTS

1 pint fresh raspberries or 1 box
    (10 ounces) frozen raspberries in
    syrup, thawed
Grated rind of 1 orange
2 tablespoons confectioners' sugar
    (for fresh raspberries)
1 tablespoon Grand Marnier or other
    orange liqueur
1 cup heavy cream

4 chewy macaroons, broken into tiny
    pieces
½ cup heavy cream, stiffly whipped,
    for decoration

If using fresh raspberries, reserve 6 of them for the garnish. Put the remaining berries on a plate with the orange rind and confectioners' sugar. If using frozen raspberries, drain them in a sieve set over a bowl. Pile the berries onto a plate with the orange rind.

In both cases, mash the berries with a fork ①, adding orange liqueur to them. Add 2 tablespoons of the syrup to the frozen berries.

Whip the cream until it holds stiff peaks and fold in the berry mixture with the crushed macaroons, just until they are mixed ②.

Divide the mixture among 6 stemmed glasses and use a pastry bag and star tip to pipe a rosette on the top of each glass ③. Use the reserved 6 fresh raspberries, if available, to garnish the rosettes. Refrigerate for 30 minutes before serving with additional macaroons or crisp cookies.

Ginger-Frosted Fruit

YIELD

4 servings

Per serving
calories 212, protein 3 g,
fat 2 g, sodium 37 mg,
carbohydrates 48 g,
potassium 854 mg

TIME

15 minutes preparation
2 hours chilling

INGREDIENTS

1 cup plain yogurt
¼ cup chopped crystallized ginger
2–3 tablespoons honey
1 teaspoon lemon juice
4 cups sliced mixed fresh fruits
   (strawberries, bananas, oranges,
   and so on)
4 sprigs mint

In a bowl, combine yogurt, ginger, honey, and lemon juice; mix thoroughly ①.

Pour mixture over fruits ② and cover. Refrigerate for at least 2 hours to marry flavors.

To serve, spoon fruits into small dessert dishes or parfait glasses. Garnish with a sprig of mint.

Ice Cream Bombe

YIELD

8 servings

Per serving (without
sauce)

calories 327, protein 4 g,
fat 21 g, sodium 102 mg,
carbohydrates 30 g,
potassium 237 mg

TIME

20 minutes preparation
5½ hours freezing

INGREDIENTS

1 quart coffee ice cream
1 pint chocolate ice cream
¾ cup heavy cream
1 tablespoon confectioners sugar
2 tablespoons creme de cacao
1 ounce semisweet chocolate, chopped
Hot fudge sauce

Place a 7-cup ice cream mold in freezer. Place coffee ice cream in re-frigerator about 20 minutes or until slightly softened. Remove mold from freezer and ice cream from refrigerator. Stir coffee ice cream until smooth and spread into mold, leaving a well in center ①. Place in freezer for 1 hour or until firm.

Place chocolate ice cream in refrigerator about 10 minutes or until slightly softened; stir until smooth. Spread over coffee ice cream in mold, leaving a well in center. Freeze 1 hour or until firm.

Whip cream with sugar until stiff. Fold in creme de cacao, then chopped chocolate. Spoon into center of mold. Freeze 3 hours or until firm.

To remove bombe from mold, place a warm damp cloth over mold 10 seconds. Run a knife around edge ②. Place a plate on bottom of mold and invert. Lift off mold ③. Serve with hot fudge sauce.

Fudge Cake

YIELD

8 servings

Per serving
calories 695, protein 6 g,
fat 29 g, sodium 511 mg,
carbohydrates 106 g,
potassium 170 mg

TIME

30 minutes preparation
30 minutes baking

INGREDIENTS

4 ounces semisweet chocolate,
  chopped
½ cup hot water
1¾ cups sugar
2 cups cake flour
1 teaspoon baking soda
1 teaspoon salt
½ cup butter
3 eggs
1 teaspoon vanilla extract
⅔ cup milk

FROSTING

¼ cup butter, melted
2 ounces semisweet chocolate, melted
¼ cup light cream
2 cups sifted confectioners sugar
1 teaspoon vanilla extract

Preheat oven to 350 degrees. Generously grease 2 9-inch round layer pans.

Combine chocolate and hot water in the top of a double boiler and heat until chocolate melts. Add ½ cup sugar and cook 2 minutes. Allow to cool slightly.

Sift flour with baking soda and salt. Sift 2 more times. Cream butter with remaining sugar until light. Add eggs 1 at a time, beating thoroughly after each addition. Stir in vanilla, then add flour ① alternately with milk ②, beating well. Add chocolate mixture and beat well ③. Pour batter into pans and bake 25 to 30 minutes, or until a toothpick inserted in center comes out clean. Allow to cool.

While cake cools, prepare frosting. Mix melted butter and chocolate, then add remaining ingredients and blend well. Spread cake with chocolate frosting.

Child's Birthday Cake

YIELD

12 servings

Per cookie
calories 463, protein 5 g, fat 16 g, sodium 314 mg, carbohydrates 76 g, potassium 125 mg

TIME

1 hour preparation
30 minutes baking

INGREDIENTS

3 cups sifted cake flour
2½ teaspoons baking powder
½ teaspoon salt
⅔ cup butter
1½ cups granulated sugar
2 eggs
1 teaspoon vanilla extract
1¼ cups milk

ICING

2 egg whites
1½ cups granulated sugar
¼ teaspoon cream of tartar
⅓ cup water
1 teaspoon vanilla extract

DECORATION

2 cups dessicated coconut
Food coloring
Jelly beans

Preheat the oven to 350 degrees. Lightly grease and then line with wax paper or parchment paper 2 cake pans, one a 9-inch square and the other an 8-inch round pan.

Sift together the flour, baking powder, and salt. In a large bowl, cream the butter, then add the sugar and continue to cream until mixture is light and fluffy. Add the eggs, 1 at a time, mixing well after each. Stir in the vanilla. Add the dry mixture to the creamed mixture, alternating with the milk and starting and ending with the dry mix.

Divide batter between the 2 cake pans and bake for 30 minutes or until a cake tester comes out clean. Cool on racks for 10 minutes, then remove from pans ①, peel off paper, and cool completely.

Make the icing in the top of a double boiler by combining the egg whites, sugar, cream of tartar, and water. Beat with a hand electric mixer for 1 minute, then place over hot water and cook for 7 minutes, beating constantly until the mixture is soft and glossy. Remove from the heat and add the vanilla.

Cut the square cake into a *t*-shape and remove the rectangular pieces on either side ②. Cut these in half crosswise and attach each strip onto the cross pieces of the *t* to make legs. Use the round cake for the head.

Divide the coconut into 4 small dessert dishes. Leave 1 dish uncolored and tint the others yellow, red, and blue. Pat the coconut onto the cake: yellow for the hair, blue and red for the shirt and pants, and white for the face, arms, and legs ③. Fill in the facial features with jelly beans.

Pineapple Orange Upside Down Cake

YIELD

8 servings

Per serving
calories 377, protein 4 g,
fat 17 g, sodium 372 mg,
carbohydrates 52 g,
potassium 147 mg

TIME

15 minutes preparation
35 to 40 minutes cooking
5 minutes cooling

INGREDIENTS

½ cup + 3 tablespoons butter, at
   room temperature
1 can (11 ounces) mandarin orange
   sections
1 can (8 ounces) pineapple rings
⅓ cup firmly packed light brown
   sugar
⅔ cup granulated sugar
2 eggs
½ teaspoon vanilla extract

1⅓ cups all-purpose flour
1 teaspoon baking powder
½ teaspoon salt
⅓ cup milk

Preheat oven to 350 degrees. Place 3 tablespoons butter in a 9-inch round cake pan. Place pan in oven until butter is melted. Drain oranges and pineapple slices on paper towels ①. Arrange in bottom of pan. Sprinkle with brown sugar ②.

In medium bowl, beat remaining ½ cup butter and sugar until creamy. Add eggs and vanilla. Stir in flour, baking powder, and salt. Stir in milk. Spread batter over fruit ③. Bake 35 to 40 minutes until cake tester inserted in center comes out clean.

Let stand 5 minutes. Run a knife around edge of cake. Place a plate over cake and pan and invert. Remove pan.

Gingerbread Jelly Roll

YIELD

10 servings

Per serving
calories 292, protein 3 g,
fat 11 g, sodium 194 mg,
carbohydrates 46 g,
potassium 198 mg

TIME

20 minutes preparation
25 minutes cooking
1 hour cooling

INGREDIENTS

½ cup + 3 tablespoons granulated
  sugar
1 cup all-purpose flour
1¼ teaspoons baking soda
¼ teaspoon salt
3 egg yolks
¼ cup butter, melted
¼ cup molasses
2 tablespoons water
1 tablespoon ground ginger
2 teaspoons ground cinnamon
1 teaspoon ground cloves
3 egg whites

FILLING

6 cups chopped, pared apples (4 large
  apples)
¼ cup butter
½ teaspoon ground cinnamon
⅓ cup granulated sugar
¼ cup water

Preheat oven to 375 degrees. Grease a 17 × 11 × 1-inch jellyroll pan. Line with waxed paper. Grease waxed paper and sprinkle with 1 tablespoon sugar and 1 tablespoon flour.

Sift together remaining flour, baking soda, and salt. Beat egg yolks with the ½ cup sugar, melted butter, molasses, water, ginger, cinnamon, and cloves until thick about 3 minutes. Fold in flour mixture.

Beat egg whites until stiff. Fold into batter. Spread into prepared pan. Bake 12 minutes until firm to the touch. While cake is baking, sprinkle a clean kitchen towel with 1 tablespoon sugar.

Let cake stand 1 minute. Loosen edges from pan and invert cake onto towel. Peel off waxed paper ① (if cake sticks, slide a knife between cake and waxed paper to separate). Sprinkle top of cake with 1 tablespoon sugar. Roll up cake and towel ②. Place seam side down on wire rack and cool completely.

For filling, mix all ingredients in medium saucepan. Cover and cook over medium-low heat, stirring occasionally, 12 to 15 minutes until tender. Uncover and cook, stirring constantly to break up pieces of apple, 3 to 5 minutes until liquid has evaporated. Cool.

Unroll cake. Spread with apple mixture ③. Reroll cake, removing towel. Refrigerate until serving time.

Cinnamon Cheesecake

YIELD

10 servings

Per serving
calories 413, protein 7 g,
fat 26 g, sodium 233 mg,
carbohydrates 37 g,
potassium 146 mg

TIME

10 minutes preparation
1 hour, 10 minutes
    cooking
5 hours setting

INGREDIENTS

1¼ cups granola
16 ounces cream cheese, at room
    temperature
1 cup granulated sugar
1 tablespoon vanilla extract
1 teaspoon ground cinnamon
¼ teaspoon salt
4 eggs
½ cup heavy cream
1 cup cherry pie filling

Preheat oven to 350 degrees. Sprinkle granola into bottom of an 8-inch springform pan. Bake 10 minutes. Reduce oven to 300 degrees. In large bowl, beat cream cheese until smooth. Beat in sugar, vanilla, cinnamon, and salt. Add eggs and heavy cream and beat until combined. Pour into springform pan ①. Bake 1 hour. Turn oven off and leave cake in oven, without opening door, 1 hour.

Remove cake from oven and let cool to room temperature. Remove side of pan ②. Spread cherry pie filling over top ③ and refrigerate several hours.

Blueberry, Peaches and Cream Tart

YIELD

10 servings

Per serving
calories 210, protein 2 g,
fat 13 g, sodium 131 mg,
carbohydrates 19 g,
potassium 100 mg

TIME

25 minutes preparation
10 to 15 minutes cooking
2½ hours chilling

INGREDIENTS

1 package (17¼ ounces) frozen puff
   pastry (will only use 1 sheet)
1 egg yolk
1 teaspoon water
½ teaspoon granulated sugar

FILLING

3 ounces cream cheese, at room
   temperature
1 tablespoon light brown sugar
1 tablespoon granulated sugar

½ teaspoon vanilla extract
⅓ cup sour cream

FRUIT AND GLAZE

2 peaches or nectarines
¼ cup apricot preserves
½ cup blueberries

Thaw 1 sheet of puff pastry according to package directions. On lightly floured surface, roll pastry into a 10-inch square ①. Cut two 1-inch strips from the bottom. Brush a 1-inch strip of pastry, on both the top and the bottom of the rectangle, with water. Lay strips of pastry over water and press lightly to attach ②. Beat egg yolk and water. Brush over pastry strips and sprinkle with sugar. Prick bottom of pastry (not strips) in several places ③. Chill 30 minutes.

Preheat oven to 400 degrees. Bake pastry on lightly greased baking sheet, 10 to 15 minutes until lightly browned. Press down center of pastry if puffed. Remove to wire rack to cool.

Beat cream cheese until smooth. Beat in brown sugar, granulated sugar, and vanilla. Stir in sour cream. Spread on cooled pastry. Cover and chill 2 hours or until firm.

Cut peaches into slices. Heat apricot preserves over low heat just until melted; strain. Arrange peaches and blueberries over cream. Brush with preserves. Refrigerate until serving time.

Lemon Cream Pie

YIELD

8 servings

Per serving
calories 258, protein 3 g,
fat 14 g, sodium 131 mg,
carbohydrates 31 g,
potassium 119 mg

TIME

15 minutes preparation
2 to 3 hours chilling

INGREDIENTS

¾ cup graham cracker crumbs
3 tablespoons granulated sugar
3 tablespoons butter, melted

⅓ cup lemon juice
1 cup plain yogurt
5 lemon slices

FILLING

1 envelope unflavored gelatin
¼ cup water
¾ cup heavy cream
⅔ cup granulated sugar
2 teaspoons grated lemon peel

In small bowl, mix graham cracker crumbs and sugar. Stir in butter ①. Press mixture into bottom of an 8-inch springform pan ②.

Sprinkle gelatin over water in small saucepan. Cook over low heat, stirring until gelatin is dissolved. Remove from heat and cool slightly.

Beat heavy cream and sugar until stiff. Stir lemon peel, lemon juice, and yogurt into gelatin. Fold lemon mixture into whipped cream ③. Turn into springform pan. Cover and refrigerate until set, 2 to 3 hours. Just before serving, cut halfway through lemon slices and garnish pie with twisted lemon slices.

French Silk Pie

YIELD

10 servings

Per serving
calories 455, protein 6 g,
fat 36 g, sodium 196 mg,
carbohydrates 32 g,
potassium 247 mg

TIME

25 minutes preparation
3 hours chilling

INGREDIENTS

⅔ cup finely chopped pecans or walnuts
⅓ cup tea cookie crumbs
¼ cup granulated sugar
¼ cup butter, melted

FILLING

½ cup butter, at room temperature
¾ cup granulated sugar
2 teaspoons vanilla extract
3 ounces unsweetened chocolate, melted

⅛ teaspoon salt
3 eggs
¼ cup sliced almonds
¼ cup chopped pecans or walnuts
¾ cup grated white chocolate (2 ounces)
½ cup pecan or walnut halves

Stir together chopped pecans, crumbs, and sugar. Stir in butter ①. Press mixture into a 9-inch pie plate.

For filling, in large bowl beat butter, sugar, and vanilla until light and fluffy. Beat in chocolate and salt. Add eggs, one at a time, beating 3 minutes after each egg ②. Stir in almonds and pecans. Fold in white chocolate. Spoon mixture into pie shell, mounding in center ③. Cover and refrigerate several hours. Garnish with pecan halves.

Pecan Pie

YIELD

6 servings

Per serving (without topping)

calories 839, protein 10 g, fat 44 g, sodium 313 mg, carbohydrates 106 g, potassium 254 mg

TIME

25 minutes preparation
1 hour chilling
35 to 40 minutes baking

INGREDIENTS

1½ cups sifted all-purpose flour
½ cup butter, softened
4 eggs + 1 egg yolk
2 tablespoons ice water, approximately
2 cups dark corn syrup
2 tablespoons butter, melted and cooled
1 teaspoon vanilla extract
1½ cups pecan halves (about 6 ounces)
Whipped cream or ice cream

Preheat oven to 400 degrees.

Place flour in a mixing bowl; make a well in center and add butter, egg yolk, and ice water ①. Mix until well blended and dough sticks together. Shape into a ball ② and chill 30 minutes before rolling out.

Roll out dough and line a 10-inch pie plate, decorating edges with tines of a fork ③. Chill pie shell for 30 minutes. Preheat oven to 350 degrees.

Beat eggs in a mixing bowl until smooth. Beating constantly, add corn syrup in a slow stream. Add melted butter and vanilla and beat until well blended. Pour egg mixture into the pie shell and scatter or arrange pecan halves over the top. Bake in middle of oven for 35 to 40 minutes, or until filling is firm. Serve warm with cream or ice cream.

Apple Raisin Turnovers

YIELD

8 turnovers

Per turnover
calories 341, protein 3 g,
fat 22 g, sodium 254 mg,
carbohydrates 33 g,
potassium 134 mg

TIME

20 minutes preparation
25 minutes cooking
30 minutes cooling

INGREDIENTS

1 package (17¼ ounces) frozen puff
   pastry
2 large apples
¼ teaspoon vanilla extract
2 tablespoons light brown sugar
¼ teaspoon ground cinnamon
⅓ cup raisins
1½ teaspoons granulated sugar
Pinch of ground cinnamon
1 tablespoon milk

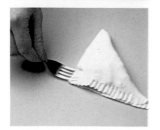

Thaw pastry according to package directions. Preheat oven to 375 degrees. While pastry is thawing, pare, core, and chop apples. Sprinkle with vanilla and mix. Stir together brown sugar and cinnamon. Add apples and raisins to sugar mixture and toss to coat apples evenly with mixture.

On lightly floured surface, unfold pastry. Cut each sheet into quarters. Place about ⅛ cup apple mixture onto each piece of pastry ①. Fold pastry in half over apple mixture, forming a triangle ②. Press edges together and, using fork tines, seal closed ③. Make 3 small slices in top of each for vent.

Mix sugar and pinch of cinnamon. Brush each turnover with milk and sprinkle lightly with cinnamon sugar. Bake on very lightly greased baking sheet about 25 minutes until lightly browned. Cool on wire racks.

Prune-Walnut Bread

YIELD

1 loaf, about 12 slices

Per slice
calories 283, protein 5 g,
fat 14 g, sodium 157 mg,
carbohydrates 36 g, potassium
214 mg

TIME

15 minutes preparation
50 to 60 minutes baking

INGREDIENTS

1½ cups all-purpose flour
⅔ cup granulated sugar
½ cup wheat germ
1¼ teaspoons apple pie spice
1 teaspoon baking soda
¼ teaspoon salt
½ cup butter, cut into chunks
2 eggs
½ cup sour cream
1 cup diced pitted prunes
½ cup chopped walnuts

Preheat the oven to 375 degrees. Lightly grease an 8½-by-4-inch baking pan or loaf pan.

In a large bowl combine the flour, sugar, wheat germ, apple pie spice, baking soda, and salt. Add the butter and, using a pastry blender, 2 knives, or your fingers, cut in until the mixture resembles coarse meal ①.

In a small bowl combine the eggs and sour cream. Blend into the flour mixture ②, then stir in the prunes and walnuts until just mixed. Spoon the batter into the baking pan ③ and bake for 50 to 60 minutes or until a cake tester comes out clean. Allow to cool in the pan for 10 minutes, then remove cake and cool completely on a rack. Serve warm or cooled with butter or cream cheese, if desired.

Cranberry Muffins

YIELD
12

Per serving
calories 187, protein 3 g,
fat 8 g, sodium 123 mg,
carbohydrates 26 g, potassium
81 mg

TIME
15 minutes preparation
20 minutes baking

INGREDIENTS
2¼ cups all-purpose flour
¾ cup granulated sugar
1 teaspoon baking soda
¼ teaspoon salt
1 egg, slightly beaten
1¼ cups buttermilk
4 tablespoons butter, melted
1 cup chopped cranberries
½ cup chopped pecans or walnuts
Confectioners' sugar

Preheat the oven to 400 degrees. Lightly grease a muffin tin or fill cupcake tins with paper liners.

In a large bowl combine the flour, ¼ cup sugar, baking soda, and salt. Toss lightly with a fork ①.

In a small bowl, combine the egg, buttermilk, and butter and blend well. Add to the dry ingredients and stir just enough to moisten ②.

Toss the cranberries with the remaining sugar and add to the batter, along with the chopped nuts. Spoon batter into the muffin or cupcake tins, filling them two-thirds full ③. Bake for 20 minutes, or until a cake tester comes out clean. Sprinkle with confectioners' sugar and serve warm.

Old-Fashioned Sugar Cookies

YIELD

5 to 6 dozen

Per cookie (5 dozen)
calories 81, protein 1 g, fat 5 g,
sodium 60 mg, carbohydrates
11 g, potassium 14 mg

TIME

10 to 15 minutes
 preparation
2 to 3 hours chilling
10 to 12 minutes baking

INGREDIENTS

4 cups all-purpose flour
1 teaspoon baking powder
½ teaspoon baking soda
½ teaspoon salt
½ teaspoon ground nutmeg
1 tablespoon grated lemon rind
1 cup butter, softened
1¼ cups granulated sugar
1 egg
¾ cup sour cream
1 teaspoon vanilla extract

In a medium bowl combine the flour, baking powder, baking soda, salt, nutmeg, and lemon rind. Toss lightly with a fork to mix.

In a large bowl cream the butter and sugar until light and fluffy. Add the egg, sour cream, and vanilla and combine well. Add the flour mixture to the creamed mixture and mix well. Refrigerate 2 to 3 hours.

Preheat the oven to 375 degrees. Lightly grease a cookie sheet.

Roll out one quarter of the dough at a time onto a lightly floured surface. Roll until ¼ inch thick, then cut with floured cookie cutters ①. Roll and cut remaining dough. Reroll and cut scraps. Transfer cookies to the cookie sheet using a broad spatula, and bake for 10 to 12 minutes, or until cookies are lightly browned. Cool completely on a rack.

VARIATIONS *Brush the uncooked cookies with slightly beaten egg white ② and sprinkle with colored sugar, sprinkles, or jimmies ③. Or place a walnut or pecan half in the center of each cookie before baking.*

Monster Chocolate Chip Cookies

YIELD

18 giant cookies

Per cookie

calories 325, protein 3 g, fat 18 g, sodium 105 mg, carbohydrates 40 g, potassium 119 mg

TIME

10 minutes preparation
12 to 14 minutes baking

INGREDIENTS

¾ cup granulated sugar
¾ cup firmly packed brown sugar
½ cup butter, softened
½ cup vegetable shortening
2 eggs
1 teaspoon vanilla extract
2¼ cups all-purpose flour
1 teaspoon baking soda

1 teaspoon cream of tartar
¼ teaspoon salt
12 ounces (2 cups) semisweet chocolate morsels
Granulated sugar

Preheat the oven to 350 degrees. Lightly grease a cookie sheet.

In a mixing bowl cream the sugars with the butter and shortening until light and fluffy. Add the eggs 1 at a time, beating well after each addition. Stir in vanilla.

Sift together the flour, baking soda, cream of tartar, and salt and add to the sugar mixture, beating well. Fold in the chocolate chips.

Form ¼ cup of batter into a ball ① and roll it in the granulated sugar ②. Place on the cookie sheet and, with the fingertips, press into a 4-inch circle ③. Bake for 12 to 14 minutes, or until cookie springs back when pressed on top. Cool on sheet for 1 minute before removing to a rack to cool completely.

Peanut and Jelly Cookies

YIELD

3 dozen

Per cookie

calories 70, protein 1 g, fat 4 g, sodium 29 mg, carbohydrates 8 g, potassium 33 mg

TIME

15 minutes preparation
25 minutes baking

INGREDIENTS

½ cup butter, softened
¼ cup firmly packed dark brown
  sugar
1 egg, separated
1 cup all-purpose flour
1 cup finely chopped unsalted peanuts
½ cup grape jelly

Preheat the oven to 300 degrees. Lightly grease a cookie sheet.

In a medium bowl cream the butter and brown sugar until light and fluffy. Add the egg yolk, then the flour and beat until well blended.

Lightly beat the egg white. Using a rounded ½ teaspoon measure of dough, form balls of dough ①. Dip each ball into the egg white and then into the chopped peanuts ②.

Place the balls on the cookie sheet and, using your fingertip, make a small depression in each one ③. Bake for 5 minutes, then remove the cookie sheet from the oven and press the centers again. Return cookies to oven and bake for an additional 20 minutes. Cool completely and fill centers with grape jelly.

Genemary's Chocolate Crack-Ups

YIELD

5 dozen

Per cookie

calories 71, protein 1 g, fat 3 g, sodium 52 mg, carbohydrates 10 g, potassium 25 mg

TIME

15 minutes preparation
3 to 4 hours chilling
8 to 10 minutes baking

INGREDIENTS

½ cup plus 1 tablespoon butter
6 tablespoons cocoa
1⅔ cups granulated sugar
2 eggs
2 teaspoons vanilla extract
2 cups all-purpose flour
½ teaspoon salt
2 teaspoons baking powder
1 cup coarsely chopped walnuts
Confectioners' sugar

Preheat the oven to 350 degrees.

Melt the butter and stir in the cocoa; blend well, then cool. Add the sugar, eggs, and vanilla, and beat until smooth.

In a separate bowl sift together the flour, salt, and baking powder. Add to the cocoa mixture ①, then add the walnuts. Chill for at least 3 hours.

Take 1 teaspoon of dough and shape it into a ball ②. Use the rest of the dough to make the remaining balls. Roll balls in confectioners' sugar ③, then place on an ungreased cookie sheet and bake for 8 to 10 minutes. Remove from oven as soon as they are set; the centers should be moist. Cool.

NOTE Cookies should be soft and chewy inside like a brownie.

Figgy Newtons

YIELD

32 bars

Per cookie
calories 135, protein 2 g,
fat 4 g, sodium 57 mg,
carbohydrates 26 g, potassium
118 mg

TIME

30 minutes preparation
20 minutes chilling
15 to 18 minutes baking

INGREDIENTS

1¼ cups whole-wheat flour
1¼ cups all-purpose flour
¼ teaspoon baking soda
¼ teaspoon salt
½ cup butter, softened
1 cup granulated sugar
2 eggs
1 teaspoon vanilla extract

FILLING

1 pound dried figs
⅓ cup granulated sugar
½ cup water
1 teaspoon grated lemon rind

In a large bowl combine the whole-wheat and all-purpose flours. Stir in the baking soda and salt.

Cream the butter and sugar until light and fluffy. Add the eggs and vanilla and mix well. Add the dry ingredients and stir until well blended. Chill while making the filling.

Chop the figs in a meat grinder or food processor. Add the sugar, water, and lemon rind. Place in a medium saucepan and simmer for 5 minutes to thicken. Cool. Lightly grease a cookie sheet.

On a lightly floured surface or between 2 sheets of wax paper, roll out half the dough into an 8 by 16-inch rectangle. Cut lengthwise into 2 strips, each 4 by 16 inches. Place one quarter of the fig mixture evenly down the center of each strip ①. Fold the sides of the dough over the filling and press edges lightly ②.

Flip the strips over with a broad spatula and cut in half ③. Transfer to the cookie sheet and chill for 20 minutes.

Preheat the oven to 375 degrees.

Bake cookies for 15 to 18 minutes or until lightly browned. Cut into 2-inch lengths while still warm using a sharp knife, then cool.

Chocolate Lace Cookies

YIELD

3 dozen

Per cookie
calories 97, protein 1 g, fat 6 g,
sodium 30 mg, carbohydrates
10 g, potassium 49 mg

TIME

30 minutes preparation
8 to 10 minutes baking

INGREDIENTS

⅔ cup granulated sugar
½ cup butter
2 tablespoons light corn syrup
2 tablespoons milk
1 cup sliced almonds
½ cup all-purpose flour
2 tablespoons finely chopped candied
    cherries
2 tablespoons finely minced citron or
    orange rind
½ teaspoon vanilla extract
1 cup semisweet chocolate morsels

Preheat the oven to 350 degrees. Cover a cookie sheet with aluminum foil, then lightly butter and flour the sheet.

In a medium saucepan combine the sugar, butter, corn syrup, and milk. Over medium heat cook to 232 degrees on a candy thermometer (soft ball stage).

Remove from the heat and stir in almonds, flour, candied fruits, and vanilla. Mix well. Drop by teaspoonfuls onto the cookie sheet ①, allowing about 4 inches of space between the cookies. Bake for 8 to 10 minutes, or until brown around the edges. Peel cookies off foil and cool completely.

Heat the chocolate chips over hot (*not* boiling) water until melted. Spread the bottom side of each cookie with melted chocolate ② and place on a wire rack to harden ③. If desired, draw a decorating comb or other clean comb over the chocolate to form swirls.

NOTE *Do not attempt to make these cookies on an exceptionally damp day. They will remain sticky when removed from oven.*

Chocolate Linzer Cookies

YIELD

9 filled cookies

Per cookie
calories 335, protein 5 g,
fat 15 g, sodium 114 mg,
carbohydrates 48 g, potassium
113 mg

TIME

20 minutes preparation
4 to 5 hours chilling
8 to 10 minutes baking

INGREDIENTS

1½ cups all-purpose flour
1 tablespoon sifted cocoa
1 teaspoon ground cinnamon
¾ cup granulated sugar
½ cup ground shelled almonds
½ cup butter, cut into pieces
1 egg
½ cup raspberry or apricot jam
Confectioners' sugar

In a medium bowl combine the flour, cocoa, cinnamon, sugar, and almonds. Toss lightly with a fork, add the butter pieces, and cut in with a pastry blender or use your fingertips. Stir in the egg and mix completely. Gather into a ball. Wrap securely in plastic wrap and chill for 4 to 5 hours.

Preheat the oven to 350 degrees.

On a lightly floured surface roll out half the dough until ¼ inch thick. Cut out rounds using a 3-inch biscuit cutter. With the remaining half of the dough cut out rounds with the same cutter, but cut a smaller circle (about ¾ inch) in the center ①, using a bottle cap.

Place both batches on an ungreased cookie sheet and bake for 8 to 10 minutes. Remove from the cookie sheet and cool completely.

Spread the plain cookies with raspberry or apricot jam ② and cover with a cookie with a hole in the center ③. Sprinkle tops with confectioners' sugar.

Surprise Kisses

YIELD

3 to 4 dozen

Per cookie

calories 141, protein 2 g,
fat 9 g, sodium 55 mg,
carbohydrates 14 g, potassium
48 mg

TIME

15 minutes preparation
7 to 10 minutes baking

INGREDIENTS

1 cup butter, softened
½ cup granulated sugar
1 teaspoon vanilla extract
2⅓ cups all-purpose flour
¾ cup finely chopped nuts
36 to 48 milk chocolate Kisses
Confectioners' sugar

Preheat the oven to 375 degrees.

Cream the butter, sugar, and vanilla in a large mixer bowl until light and fluffy ①. Add the flour and chopped nuts; blend well.

Remove the foil from the candies.

Shape about 1 tablespoon of dough around each candy ②, covering it completely. Place on an ungreased cookie sheet and bake for 7 to 10 minutes or until set but not brown.

Cool; roll in confectioners' sugar ③, and store in an airtight container. Roll in sugar again before serving.

Three-Layer Brownies

YIELD

20 brownies

Per brownie

calories 313, protein 4 g,
fat 15 g, sodium 131 mg,
carbohydrates 42 g,
potassium 123 mg

TIME

20 minutes preparation
35 to 40 minutes cooking
1 hour cooling

INGREDIENTS

3 ounces unsweetened chocolate
⅔ cup butter
3 eggs
1½ cups granulated sugar
2 teaspoons vanilla extract
1 cup all-purpose flour

BUTTERSCOTCH LAYER

¼ cup butter, at room temperature
3 ounces cream cheese, at room
    temperature

1 cup firmly packed dark brown sugar
2 eggs
2 teaspoons vanilla extract
⅔ cup all-purpose flour

ICING

1 ounce unsweetened chocolate
2 tablespoons butter
1 cup confectioners sugar
2 tablespoons milk

Preheat oven to 375 degrees. Grease and flour a 9 × 13-inch pan. Melt chocolate and butter over low heat. In medium bowl, beat eggs, sugar and vanilla. Beat in melted chocolate mixture ①. Stir in flour until well combined.

For butterscotch layer, beat butter and cream cheese until smooth; beat in brown sugar. Beat in eggs and vanilla. Stir in flour.

Spread brownies into pan. Pour butterscotch mixture over brownies and spread evenly ②. Bake 35 to 40 minutes; cool on wire rack.

For icing, melt chocolate and butter over low heat. In small bowl, stir together confectioners sugar and milk until smooth. Stir in melted chocolate mixture. Spread over brownies ③ and set aside until set. Cut into bars.

Blondies

YIELD

16 bars

Per cookie
calories 154, protein 2 g,
fat 8 g, sodium 71 mg,
carbohydrates 19 g, potassium
93 mg

TIME

10 minutes preparation
25 minutes baking

INGREDIENTS

¼ cup butter
1 cup firmly packed light brown sugar
1 egg
¾ cup all-purpose flour
1 teaspoon baking powder
Dash of salt
1 teaspoon vanilla extract
1 cup chopped walnuts

Preheat the oven to 350 degrees. Generously grease an 8-inch square baking pan.

Melt the butter and add the brown sugar. Cook, stirring constantly, for 30 seconds or until well blended. Cool, then add the egg.

Combine the flour, baking powder, and salt and add to the brown sugar mixture ①. Stir in the vanilla and walnuts, then spread in the baking pan ②. Bake for 25 minutes, or until a toothpick inserted in the center comes out clean ③. Cool and cut into squares.

Apricot Bars

YIELD

18 bar cookies

Per cookie
calories 192, protein 2 g,
fat 8 g, sodium 113 mg,
carbohydrates 30 g,
potassium 43 mg

TIME

15 minutes preparation
35 to 40 minutes cooking

INGREDIENTS

³/₄ cup butter, at room temperature
½ cup granulated sugar
⅓ cup firmly packed light brown
  sugar
2 cups all-purpose flour
¼ teaspoon salt
¼ teaspoon baking soda
1 tablespoon lemon juice
³/₄ cup apricot preserves

Preheat oven to 375 degrees. Grease a 9-inch square baking pan. In medium bowl, beat butter until creamy. Stir in sugar and brown sugar. Add flour, salt, and baking soda. Stir until mixture is crumbly.

Set aside 1 cup crumb mixture for top; press remaining crumb mixture into baking pan ①. Stir lemon juice into apricot preserves. Spread into pan, leaving a ¼-inch border around all edges ②.

Sprinkle preserves with remaining 1 cup crumb mixture ③. Bake 35 to 40 minutes until lightly browned.

Gingerbread People

YIELD

2 dozen, about 5 inches high

Per cookie
calories 144, protein 2 g, fat 4 g, sodium 117 mg, carbohydrates 26 g, potassium 219 mg

TIME

20 minutes preparation
2 to 3 hours chilling
8 to 10 minutes baking

INGREDIENTS

½ cup butter, softened
½ cup granulated sugar
½ cup molasses
1 egg yolk
2 cups all-purpose flour
½ teaspoon salt
1 teaspoon baking powder
½ teaspoon baking soda
1½ teaspoons ground cinnamon
1 teaspoon ground cloves

1 teaspoon ground ginger
½ teaspoon ground nutmeg

ICING

2¼ cups sifted confectioners' sugar
2 egg whites
¼ teaspoon cream of tartar

In a large bowl cream together the butter, sugar, and molasses. Add the egg yolk and mix well.

Sift together the flour, salt, baking powder, baking soda, cinnamon, cloves, ginger, and nutmeg. Stir into the molasses mixture and mix well. Chill for 2 to 3 hours.

Preheat the oven to 350 degrees.

On a lightly floured surface roll out the dough until it is ¼ inch thick ①. Cut with gingerbread boy and girl cutters ②. Place cookies on an ungreased cookie sheet and bake for 8 to 10 minutes or until cookies spring back when depressed slightly. Cool on a rack.

With an electric mixer at high speed beat together the confectioners' sugar, egg whites, and cream of tartar until the icing holds a peak ③. Fill a decorating tube or pastry bag. Outline the cookies and mark the eyes and mouths. Allow icing to set before serving cookies or storing them.

Rosettes

YIELD

3 dozen

Per cookie

calories 75, protein 1 g, fat 6 g, sodium 38 mg, carbohydrates 5 g, potassium 18 mg

TIME

15 minutes preparation
20 minutes cooking

INGREDIENTS

2 eggs
3 tablespoons granulated sugar
1/2 teaspoon salt
2 tablespoons vegetable oil
1/2 cup evaporated milk
1/2 cup water
1 cup all-purpose flour
Vegetable shortening for deep-frying
Confectioners' sugar

Whisk together the eggs and sugar. Beat in the salt, oil, evaporated milk, water, and flour. Mixture should be smooth.

Heat the shortening to 400 degrees. Dip the rosette iron into the oil and get it hot. Drain excess oil onto paper towels.

Dip the hot iron into the batter ①, just until top of the form. (If you go over the top, the rosette will not fall off as it cooks.) Fry until golden brown ②. Turn once. Remove cookie with a 2-pronged fork ③, and drain well on paper towels. Dip iron into hot oil before dipping into batter again; repeat for each rosette. Sprinkle rosettes with confectioners' sugar. Serve warm or cool.

CREDITS

RECIPE CREDITS

Aaron, Jan: pp. 35, 37, 45, 49, 51, 53, 57, 101, 105, 147, 153, 173, 191, 201, 219, 231, 245, 247, 283

Bennett, Bev: pp. 3, 5, 7, 9, 13, 15, 17, 19, 27, 29, 31, 93, 241

Bianco, Marie: pp. 23, 121, 125, 129, 131, 135, 137, 139, 141, 155, 157, 345, 369, 387, 389, 391, 393, 395, 397, 399, 401, 403, 405, 409, 413, 415

Bond, Jules: pp. 55, 75, 107, 133, 149, 163, 167, 177, 205, 227, 229, 243, 255, 265, 269, 287, 307

Butel, Jane: pp. 11, 195, 239, 263

Chen, Pearl: p. 343

Delu, Christian: p. 321

Doubleday & Co., Inc.: p. 329

Feingold, Helen: pp. 63, 65, 67, 69, 73, 99, 103, 115, 123, 127, 183, 209, 213, 217, 221, 223, 237, 257, 261, 275, 291, 323, 341

Giusti-Lanham, Hedy and Dodi, Andrea: p. 325

Hanes, Phyllis: pp. 41, 43, 97, 117, 119, 193, 197, 207, 225, 235, 249, 253, 271, 285, 299, 301, 313, 331, 367, 383

Julian, Sheryl: pp. 21, 25, 45, 77, 143, 151, 169, 179, 181, 203, 215, 259, 273, 277, 297, 303, 309, 315, 317, 333, 357, 361

Koury, Christine: pp. 355, 359, 365, 371, 373, 375, 377, 379, 381, 385, 407, 411

Mitchell, Susan: pp. 39, 59, 71, 113, 161, 165, 171, 185, 279, 281, 295, 305, 337, 347, 363

Olney, Judith: p. 327

Sarlin, Janeen: pp. 79, 81, 83, 85, 87, 89, 91, 175

Upton, Kim: pp. 3, 5, 7, 9, 13, 15, 17, 19, 27, 29, 31, 93, 241

Weinstein, Norman: pp. 109, 111, 145, 187, 189, 199, 233, 267, 293, 311

PHOTO CREDITS

Helms, Bill: pp. 98-99, 126-127, 208-209, 212-213, 216-217, 222-223, 236-237, 256-257, 260-261, 274-275, 290-291, 306-307

Horowitz, Irwin: pp. 2-3, 4-5, 6-7, 8-9, 12-13, 14-15, 16-17, 18-19, 20-21, 22-23, 24-25, 26-27, 28-29, 30-31, 44-45, 76-77, 108-109, 110-111, 120-121, 124-125, 128-129, 130-131, 134-135, 136-137, 138-139, 140-141, 142-143, 144-145, 150-151, 154-155, 156-157, 168-169, 178-179, 180-181, 186-187, 188-189, 198-199, 202-203, 214-215, 232-233, 258-259, 266-267, 272-273, 276-277, 292-293, 296-297, 302-303, 308-309, 310-311, 314-315, 316-317, 320-321, 324-325, 326-327, 328-329, 332-333, 342-343, 344-345, 356-357, 360-361, 368-369, 386-387, 388-389, 390-391, 392-393, 394-395, 396-397, 398-399, 400-401, 402-403, 404-405, 408-409, 412-413, 414-415

Klein, Matthew: pp. 10-11, 34-35, 36-37, 38-39, 44-45, 48-49, 50-51, 52-53, 56-57, 58-59, 62-63, 64-65, 66-67, 68-69, 70-71, 72-73, 78-79, 80-81, 82-83, 84-85, 86-87, 88-89, 90-91, 92-93, 100-101, 102-103, 104-105, 112-113, 114-115, 122-123, 146-147, 152-153, 160-161, 164-165, 170-171, 172-173, 174-175, 182-183, 184-185, 190-191, 194-195, 200-201, 218-219, 220-211, 230-231, 238-239, 240-241, 244-245, 246-247, 262-263, 278-279, 280-281, 282-283, 294-295, 304-305, 322-323, 336-337, 340-341, 346-347, 354-355, 358-359, 362-363, 364-365, 370-371, 372-373, 374-375, 376-377, 378-379, 380-381, 384-385, 406-407, 410-411

Leeds, Karen: pp. 40-41, 42-43, 54-55, 74-75, 96-97, 106-107, 116-117, 118-119, 132-133, 148-149, 162-163, 166-167, 176-177, 192-193, 196-197, 204-205, 206-207, 224-225, 226-227, 228-229, 234-235, 242-243, 248-249, 252-253, 254-255, 264-265, 268-269, 270-271, 284-285, 286-287, 298-299, 300-301, 306-307, 312-313, 330-331, 366-367, 382-383

RECIPE INDEX